A Parent's Guide to Standardized Tests in School

How to Improve Your Child's Chances for Success

Peter W. Cookson, Jr., Ph.D.

Joshua Halberstam, Ph.D.

Teachers College Columbia University

with

Kristina Berger and Susan Mescavage

LearningExpress

NEW YORK

Library of Congress Cataloging-in-Publication Data:

Cookson, Peter W.
   A parent's guide to standardized tests in school: how to improve your child's chances for success / Peter W. Cookson, Jr., Joshua Halberstam.
      p.   cm.
   Includes bibliographical references (p.   ).
   ISBN: 1–57685–137–0
   1. Educational tests and measurements—United States.   2. Education—Parent participation—United States.   I. Halberstam, Joshua, 1946–   . II. Title.
LB3051.C638   1998
371.26′2—DC21   98-26819
                                                                               CIP

Printed in the United States of America
9 8 7 6 5 4 3 2 1
First Edition

For further information

For information on LearningExpress, other LearningExpress products, or bulk sales, please call or write to us at:
   LearningExpress™
   900 Broadway
   Suite 604
   New York, NY 10003
   212-995-2566

Regarding the Information in this Book
The information in this book is based on comprehensive, current research. Because standardized testing is a fast-changing area, however, parents are encouraged to make the most of the resources listed in this book to make sure they have up-to-date information.

 LearningExpress is an affiliated company of Random House, Inc.

Distributed to the retail trade by Random House, Inc., as agent for LearningExpress, LLC.

Visit LearningExpress on the World Wide Web at www.learnx.com.

ISBN: 1–57685–137–0

7   85555 85137   5

Acknowledgments

Only a genuine team effort could have produced this book, flush as it is with charts, sample test questions, web resources, and CD-ROM reviews, along with the more traditional writing of most books. We were especially lucky to have benefited from the wonderful support of the talented individuals who helped make this book happen.

A special thanks to:

◆ Tom Evans, for his early and sustained enthusiasm for this project;

◆ Katie Embree, Associate Director at the Center for Educational Outreach and Innovation at Teachers College, for her support at every step of this project and her vital sense of humor;

◆ Jim Gish, editor extraordinaire at LearningExpress for his expertise and gentle supervision; and

◆ Amie Jackowski of LearningExpress, for charting her way through our charts.

We'd also like to extend our gratitude to Susan Mescavage and Kristina Berger, whose research, writing, and devotion to this book were essential to its development and completion.

Contents

APPENDIXES

Foreword

Every child and family in the United States is deeply affected by testing. Test scores determine a child's educational future as well as a child's sense of well-being and worth. As we point out in this book, American children take more than 100 million standardized tests every year.

We have written *A Parent's Guide to Standardized Tests in School* because we believe that accurate and accessible information is the family's best resource for ensuring that their child's testing experience is positive and educationally productive. We also believe that this book will be useful for teachers and other educators. Because many families and even many teachers are not entirely aware of the testing process, there is widespread confusion and mistrust concerning standardized testing and the best way to prepare for these exams. It is our hope that this book will bring families and schools together.

The United States is not the only country that is relying increasingly on standardized tests to assess their children's abilities and achievements. Standardized tests are used around the world and, as you know, very often American children do not compete well with children from other countries. As part of our professional work, we have a deep interest in the many political and theoretical issues concerning standardized testing and its use as a means to rate children and improve our educational systems. This book is a welcome opportunity for us to apply our research and analysis to the real world of families and children.

We want every child in the United States to have a fair opportunity for success on standardized tests. That is why this book is pointedly practical, informative, and focused on your child. Standardized tests should be treated as challenges, not obstacles. We hope this book will help you help your child meet these challenges—and make the most of the educational opportunities ahead.

Peter W. Cookson, Jr.
Joshua Halberstam

Chapter 1

◆

The New Reality of Standardized Testing

Your child will take exams this year. Lots of them. That's not new, of course. You can remember (though probably not with much joy) the parade of tests you suffered through back when you were in school. What *is* new is the kinds of tests that students are now given and the sheer number of them. In addition to the regular dosage of quizzes based on material covered in class—the kind of exams your teacher, Mrs. Terror, gleefully hurled at you—your child is also subject to a rapidly growing number of standardized tests.

"Subject to" is an understatement. In fact, American children are the most tested kids in the world, taking more than *100 million* standardized tests every year!

Whether these standardized tests measure what they claim to measure is the subject of an ongoing and heated debate. All the experts agree, though, and the research overwhelmingly confirms, that parental involvement has a significant impact on how well children learn and how well they perform on exams. In other words, what you do or don't do matters a great deal. So if you didn't already have enough responsibilities, here's something new to worry about.

It's also the reason we wrote this book. Parents can turn this "burden" into a rewarding opportunity. But to do that they need accurate, accessible, practical information. And that's what you'll find in the chapters ahead.

A Practical Guide for Parents

At the outset, we want to be as explicit as we can about the parental focus of this book. You aren't just a parent, of course. You're also a concerned citizen and an active member of your community. You might have strong opinions about the current debate on standardized tests and its consequences for the future of education and our nation. We certainly hope you voice those opinions. You can also bet that as professional educators and professors who like to profess, we, too, have our own (actually split) perspectives on the value of these exams.

But these viewpoints and the larger political issues are not our immediate concern here. For better or worse, standardized tests are a growing reality, and that reality is what we have to address. So even the brief overviews you'll find here of the historical background of standardized tests, the current debate, and the testing business are included with the same underlying purpose in mind: to provide the information you need to help your child with the standardized tests he or she will take this year and in the years to come.

WHAT IS A STANDARDIZED TEST?

Here's a straightforward definition: a standardized test is an exam that is administered in the same testing conditions to different groups. In other words, a standardized test, wherever and whenever it is given, includes the same questions, takes the same amount of time to complete, and is scored in the same way. Because of this uniformity, standardized test scores are able to show how your child did compared with others who took the test, not just in the same classroom but across the state and across the country.

A key point to bear in mind is that your child's teacher does not make up these tests. Nor does the school. Standardized tests, in most cases, are created and administered by private companies. More about this later.

A Few Key Terms

In truth, not much about standardized tests is standard. American schools now use hundreds of different standardized tests—different tests for different grades for different purposes. Still, these tests tend to fall into one of two general categories.

The first category encompasses *aptitude* tests. Their purpose is to measure inherent capability in order to predict how a student will do in the future. IQ tests are a well-known example of an aptitude test.

The mind is not a vessel to be filled but a fire to be kindled.
—Plutarch

A second category is *achievement* tests. These exams are designed to gauge what students have actually learned—how well they've mastered skills such as reading or math as appropriate for their grade level. A popular example of this kind of test is the Stanford Achievement Test.

Here's another important distinction between standardized tests: some are *norm-referenced*, which means that the student's score is compared with a select group called "the norm group." Half the kids do better than the norm, half do worse. Others are *criterion-referenced*. These tests are designed to rate a student's performance as compared with some predetermined standard—everyone can do well or everyone can do poorly.

We'll explain the difference between these kinds of tests in more detail when we look at sample questions from actual standardized tests in Chapter 4. And we'll also show you how to help your child prepare for both test types and how to analyze the results.

Change Is Everywhere

Your child will almost certainly take various forms of standardized tests this year and in the years ahead. We say "almost certainly" to hedge our bets, because right now test requirements are in flux in school districts across the country. Some states are big on testing and want to see their students tested regularly throughout elementary, junior high, and high school. Other states restrict testing to a few age groups. Some standardized tests, moreover, are given only to a randomly selected number of children.

The decision about what specific tests your child will take this year depends on the school district she attends, the school she attends within the district, and her grade level. In fact, at the beginning of the school year, even your child's teacher and school principal may not know what has been decided.

The attempt by the states and the federal government to impose some uniformity on this testing kaleidoscope has generated intense controversy. To become an informed parent—and to deal knowledgeably with your child's school—you need to be aware of the basic arguments in this debate.

A BRIEF HISTORY

Public schools trace their roots to the very beginnings of our nation. In the 1600s, Puritans in the Massachusetts Bay Colony established schools to train a new generation of ministers. (They charged tuition, and, of course, excluded females.) By 1918, essentially secular education for all children ages 6-12 was compulsory in all states. From the outset, nearly all school tests were prepared and given by the teacher to see how well students were doing with their class work.

Segue to the 1950s, a time of Cold War and mass alarm. In 1957, the Russians sent up Sputnik, the first satellite to orbit the earth, and a shocked America was caught flatfooted. The nation concluded that not only were we losing the race to space but, unless we redoubled our efforts to educate our children, especially in the sciences, we were on our way to becoming a second-rate technological power. This prompted a national effort to improve math and science education in our schools.

By the 1970s, the push for higher national standards had dissipated and the trend was now running in the opposite direction—toward liberalized education and an appreciation of decentralized learning with diverse educational goals. Standardized tests were still given, but the results didn't count much in judging school districts, schools, and students.

The Standards Movement and National Testing

In 1983, the panic mode returned. The release of a national report on the state of American education, "A Nation at Risk," concluded that our educational system was failing significantly. If this pattern were to continue, warned the report's authors, the United States was in danger of losing its already-slim competitive edge, and its citizens would be unprepared to fill highly skilled jobs. The impression of a failing school system was reinforced by the poor performance of American students in tests compared with students in other developed countries, especially in older grades, and especially in math and science.

In response, President Bush instituted a project called "Goals 2000/Educate America," which included a call for the adoption of national standards. In the early 1990s, Bush proposed compulsory national tests as part of this pursuit, but Congress rejected the idea.

President Clinton reintroduced the concept of national standards and national testing, as a keystone of his drive to improve the quality of American education. In his 1997 State of the Union Address, Clinton recommended that national tests be given for reading in the fourth grade and math in the eighth grade. (These exams are based on the National Assessment of Educational Progress, or NAEP, tests; we review them in Chapter 3.) While only a few states have been quick to comply with the President's proposal, the pursuit of national standards and national tests to measure achievement of these standards is more appealing to Americans now than perhaps ever before. But the resistance to this proposal is equally fierce.

The Current Controversy

Interestingly, opponents of national standards come from both the political right and the political left. As some wag put it, those on the right don't like anything with the word *national* in it and those on the left don't like anything with the word *test* in it.

Proponents see national standards as vital if the country takes seriously the need to upgrade our education. And national testing forces accountability on schools and gives parents the means to evaluate how their children and their children's schools are performing as compared with other children and other schools.

Those who oppose national testing say that tests don't improve education—"You cannot fatten cattle by weighing them," is how one Congressman put it. The proposed tests, mostly multiple-choice in structure, don't adequately measure genuine ability. National standards, moreover, will force teachers to "teach to the test," thereby ignoring more creative and important pedagogical goals. And educational standards, they argue, are more properly the business of the states than the federal government.

WHAT DOES ALL THIS MEAN TO YOU?

Not much, to tell the truth. If national standards are implemented, the immediate target will likely be your school's curriculum. Teachers will be encouraged to "teach to the test." But, as we've noted, whether or not your child is given a national standardized test this year, next year, or ever, he or will she will most assuredly be taking some standardized tests, and probably plenty of them.

That's the new reality of standardized testing today.

Chapter 2

Can You Really Prepare for a Standardized Test?

In theory, standardized tests, and in particular standardized aptitude tests, provide an objective measure of ability and achievement. In theory, you can't study for this type of test because you can't anticipate the questions. Indeed, for many years, ETS, the organization that produces the SAT college entrance exam, insisted that prep classes were useless. In the meantime, private companies who knew otherwise were making a mint in the private tutoring business. Can you prepare for these tests? Absolutely.

But let's be realistic. Even the most rigorous preparation isn't going to transform your child's scores from below average to genius. Nor, for that matter, will your child prodigy score in the low 10th percentile even if he or she never spends a minute getting ready for the exam. Having said that, though, there's no question that test preparation can make a significant difference in your child's performance. Moreover, planning for a standardized test is a good idea regardless of its impact on test scores. It will help to ensure that your child has a psychologically healthy response to the test and the test results.

Eventually, as these exams become routine in our schools, our children will become accustomed to standardized tests. But familiarity doesn't always equal comfort. All tests, as we know, are daunting at best, and sometimes downright scary. That's true even if you know the material well, and it's especially true of standardized tests, where you can rarely be sure of what questions will be thrown at you, or how well you're fielding those questions once the test is underway. And it sure isn't any easier when you're 10 years old.

Here, then, are some preliminary guidelines to bear in mind as you help prepare your child for an upcoming standardized test. In a later chapter, we'll review some sample tests and offer practical test-taking tips, but the immediate focus here is on the general and all-important need to develop an appropriate mental attitude toward these exams.

TEN THINGS YOU CAN DO TO HELP YOUR CHILD SUCCEED ON A STANDARDIZED TEST

1. What Test? When?

Do you think your child knows what test is coming up and when? Forget it. Be happy he remembered that they were having class pictures this morning and that it's only two weeks that he's been carrying around that note for you from his teacher. Keeping track of the standardized test schedule is *your* responsibility.

Bring up the issue early in the school year, perhaps even in your first conversation with your child's new teacher. Find out which tests your child will be taking this year and when. If you don't get an answer, ask again soon thereafter—keep asking until you do get an answer. This is information you not only have a right to know, but an obligation to know.

Write down the date in your calendar—no, not the discarded calendar in the drawer, but the one you use all the time. You want to be aware of the test at least a few weeks before the event, not a few weeks after it's over.

2. Where Are the Weak Spots?

Does you child need drilling in computation? Help with reading comprehension? Does your child have trouble following written directions? You need to determine, as honestly and intelligently as possible, the learning skills your child needs to improve most.

How do you make this determination? You don't have the time, money, or need for a thorough, independent diagnostic test (and anyway, this diagnostic information is what the standardized test is supposed to supply). Nor should you rely solely on your own assessment. A child's learning abilities go through phases, and these developments are sometimes too subtle for even attentive parents to notice. The one person you should speak to is your child's teacher.

It's the teacher's job, after all, to chart the student's intellectual progress and inform the parents about the learning skills that most need remediation. Teachers aren't infallible, of course, but parents often have set preconceptions about their children's abilities, so prepare yourself for an open, honest discussion. Ask the teacher for specific suggestions on how your child might best prepare for the upcoming test. Most teachers will be happy to accommodate. On this issue, you're both on the same side—your child's high scores make you both look good.

3. Review the Rules and Regulations

The structure of standardized tests differs from other classroom exams. The rigidity and exacting procedures of these tests, the teacher's clipped "Begin now" and emphatic "Pencils down" can be perplexing, especially to a younger child. At the end of most other class tests, your child's request for additional time—"I'm on my last question, just another second, okay?"—is granted without fuss. Not today. And when your child has difficulty understanding a test question, her teacher usually explains what is being asked of her. But during this exam the teacher is surprisingly distant and taciturn, and answers her request for more time with an official sounding "Sorry, just do the best you can."

You can diminish the tension by explaining to your child why the test environment is so demanding and her teacher is so strict about adhering to the rules. Standardized tests are reliable only to the extent that the same procedures are followed precisely everywhere. The crucial "norming" feature of the test is severely jeopardized when a class in Boise is allowed a few extra minutes to finish the test, a teacher in Richmond explains the test directions, a teacher in Fairbanks provides advice on how to answer questions in one of the test sections, while other proctors in other districts bend the rules in other ways. Standardized tests work only if they really are standard. Even 10-year-olds understand this.

4. Build Confidence

A recent acclaimed study found that 20% of early grade students underestimated their intelligence; lack of self-confidence is a serious issue with a significant portion of young children. Unfortunately, parents often exacerbate the problem. It doesn't take much, after all, for a parent to undermine a child's self-assurance. For example, a father might say, "Evan, you have that math achievement test today. This isn't a subject you're good at, is it? But, hey, you can't be good at everything, can you?" Gee, Dad, thanks for the encouragement.

There's no need to post a list of "the right words to say" to your child before an exam because your gestures can convey your pessimistic beliefs as powerfully as anything you say—a disapproving shrug or a badly timed sigh is enough to deliver the wrong message. Remember, too, that not *dis*couraging doesn't count as positive *en*couraging. Don't do nothing. Talk to your child before the test, and by all means cheer him along.

You want your child to walk into that test room feeling good about himself and his abilities . . . so help him feel that way.

5. Don't Create Unrealistic Expectations

This is the flip side of the suggestion above. Fostering unreachable goals is as bad as squelching achievable goals. If Evan really isn't a superior math student (not yet, anyway), don't try to convince him that he is. Comments like this are counterproductive: "Hey, Ev, this test will be a piece of cake. You'll breeze through it. I'm sure you'll get every question right." Evan is set up for a fall. He sits down to the test with his expectations in the stratosphere, but a minute and a half into the test he's stumped by question number three. His high spirits deflate like a punctured balloon. Evan is disappointed in himself, his confidence is shaken, and he will probably do less well than had he walked in with realistic expectations.

You want to impart to your child a balanced view of his prospects. You want him to be optimistic. But you also want him to distinguish optimism from fantasy.

6. This Is But One Test

Make sure your child understands that this is only a single test, not a final judgment of her abilities. The exam might accurately point to her areas of strength and weakness, but it is by no means a comprehensive, definitive guide to her abilities. Even luck can be a factor—although your daughter is an excellent reader, she just happened not to know the particular vocabulary words on this particular test. Perhaps she has poor test-taking skills. This works the other way too, of course—an outstanding score on this isolated test doesn't prove outstanding ability.

But you can't fake this message. Your child will take the test results in proper perspective only if you do. And you should. Because, in fact, this really *is* just one test.

7. Set Up a Study Schedule

We'll discuss in a bit how best to review sample exams, but that will be a useless exercise unless you set up a schedule for these practice sessions. And stick to it. Both you and your child will need to study together, so both of you need to make a commitment—and if you don't maintain your end of the deal, don't expect your child to be any better.

One way to "sanctify" these designated practice hours is by "sanctifying" a place in the house for your study sessions. Choose a comfortable, quiet space as your enclave and make sure everyone else in the family understands that during study time the two of you (or your child alone when he or she is studying solo) are not to be disturbed.

8. Take Care of the Test Accessories

What you don't need on the morning of the test is this all-too-commonplace scene. Your child suddenly remembers, "I need to bring two pencils. With erasers." A frantic search around the house turns up but one chewed, eraser-less pencil. It's getting late and the volume starts to rise. "Ma, I got to go. What do you mean there are no pencils in the house???" And then a new frenzy begins with the search for a calculator with working batteries, a watch, a snack.

Get ready the day before. And, may we remind you, drowsiness impairs performance, so do make sure your child gets a good night's sleep the night before the test. Hunger doesn't help one's performance, either. So even if, like most kids, your child's pre-school breakfast is usually no more than gulped-down cereal with too much sugar, this morning do better.

9. Keep Cool

We have to say this again and again: Relax. You'd appreciate the need to repeat this obvious piece of advice if you encountered as many parents as we do who are in a complete tizzy when their children take standardized tests. Our concern at the moment is less with the parent's frantic state than with the effect this has on the child: anxiety is viral and especially contagious when transmitted from parents to children.

But you don't want to sedate your child, either. Don't make your child feel guilty about feeling a bit edgy before the exam. It's only natural and, in fact, the jolt of adrenaline at test time helps keep one's attention sharp.

10. Try to Have Fun

This might sound like whistling in the dark, gallows humor, how-to book psychobabble, but you really don't need to dread standardized tests. They don't have to be painful experiences. The weighty aura of the exam is the main culprit here—if these tests were part of an adventure game on the Internet, your child would zap away with happy abandon. As we note up ahead, you should approach the practice sessions, in part, as fun, puzzle-solving games and the test in much the same spirit.

So lighten up—and get your child to lighten up as well.

STANDARDIZED TESTS AND YOUR CHILD'S LEARNING STYLE

These are general rules. But your child, of course, is not generic. He's an individual. And each child learns differently. Each absorbs and synthesizes information, in and out of school, in his own way. Your mission is to determine how your child learns best and then tailor test preparation to your child's individual learning style.

Some children, for example, learn best when they can come into physical contact with the material. They are tactile learners. Many children are visual learners, and still others understand best what they hear. And then there are those who do best when they combine various learning styles.

Let's have a closer look at these different approaches to learning.

Visual Learners

Visual learners prefer to see what they need to understand. They also lean on visual cues in recalling what they have learned. The young child who insists that she read along with the story rather than just hear it recited to her is a good example of the visual learner. Tell her what chores you expect her to do and she will later say, sincerely, that she forgot what they were, but let her read her assignments on a list and she'll remember them.

In addition to a preference for reading, visually oriented children learn by observing demonstrations, by watching productions on television and movies, and by looking at information portrayed in graphs and charts.

Test Strategies for Visual Learners

◆ Make sure your child reads the instructions before answering a test question. Given her preference for visual data, you can't be sure she will understand and remember instructions that are read to her. She needs to see them herself.

◆ Because she feels most comfortable with visual information, suggest that your child preview each test question, and look for charts or other graphical clues that might help her answer the question.

Auditory Learners

The auditory learner learns best when he hears the information. He is a good listener and remembers most clearly discussions of new material. Children with this learning style generally comprehend directions when they are spoken and don't need to read them. Indeed, they prefer to have new ideas explained to them rather than shown to them, and they assimilate information by talking it through to themselves. Not surprisingly, children with this learning style often enjoy listening to music.

Test Strategies for Auditory Learners

◆ Standardized test directions are usually read aloud. Children who lead with their ears should be cautioned to pay careful attention to the proctor's explanation of what is expected of them. The less your child relies on his reading of the directions, the more certain he can be of understanding what is required in the test.

◆ With a younger child in particular, it might be a good idea to show him how to read by moving his mouth and lips so that he actually hears what his eyes see. In this way, he focuses on the more comfortable oral aspects of the words rather than on the visual cues. Children can learn to do this quietly without annoying other children in the room.

Tactile Learners

The tactile learner is most at ease when she touches, handles, and manipulates things. This is a child who can't keep her hands off anything new. She's typically the one in the house who's most at home with the computer—she helped assemble the thing when it arrived—and has learned to surf the Net with the ease of a Southern Californian riding the waves. At school she likes to play with unifix cubes and enjoys solving math problems with the help of manipulatives such as geoboards and Beanie Bear counters.

Test Strategies for Tactile Learners

◆ Be aware: most standardized tests do not allow children to use rulers or other hands-on tools. For this reason, children who show a preference for tactile learning would benefit from learning how to be comfortable with a secondary learning style, such as visual or auditory. As part of your test preparation strategy, try to develop this ability.

◆ In the case of early graders, you might want to ask the teacher if it's okay for your child to hold on to some object in his non-writing hand: a discreet item, such as a small ball, or a soft object like Silly Putty. Having an object in his hand can help the tactile child concentrate better on the test.

◆ Help your child learn how to use drawings to aid his understanding of the material. Children who learn by manipulation can profitably use scrap paper for writing and construction. Be careful, though, that your child doesn't expend too much valuable time with these extraneous devices— work on time management.

Kinesthetic Learners

The kinesthetic learner needs concrete, hands-on experience to process new information. This is a child who learns most about volcanoes by building a lava-flowing, action-packed model. She'd learn about this subject least efficiently by reading about it in an encyclopedia. Kinesthetic learners enjoy playing games, going on trips, building things, and working on projects. Their perception is enhanced by the physicality of motion and rhythm, singing and dancing.

Test Strategies for Kinesthetic Learners

◆ Standardized tests do not provide active learning opportunities for children. It is important, therefore, for you to help your child learn how to use supplementary learning styles. Most of the learning strategies for tactile learners work for the kinesthetic learner as well.

SOME COMMON PROBLEMS

Along with individual learning styles, each child approaches tests with a distinct constellation of worries and assurances. Some kids, for example, break out into a cold sweat and their hearts begin to palpitate the moment the teacher hands them a test booklet. Other children are so self-assured that they hurry through an exam without checking their answers. This section highlights five common attitudes that can jeopardize your child's chances to score well on standardized tests—and suggests ways of addressing these problems.

The Poor Test-Taker

Poor Gerald. You review the spelling words with him the night before his test. He knows them perfectly. But then, invariably, at the test, he blows it. Letters get jumbled. He switches a K for a C, "sion" for "tion," and though he's got the "i" before "e" rule down pat, he gets it wrong on tests. To make matters worse, each time he does badly, his confidence takes another hit. Gerald, as you can imagine, is not looking forward to the upcoming standardized test.

How can you help? Often, the problem is not much deeper than a lack of test-taking skills, so try to pinpoint the tactics that your child could use but isn't. For example, review the importance of intelligent guessing—some children will not answer a question unless they are positive they know the correct answer. Shrewd guessing can dramatically increase one's score on a test.

The Test-Anxious Child

Anxiety doesn't help test performance either. It's natural to feel some anxiety before you take a test, but some children experience a level of nervousness that significantly undermines their performance. It's difficult to recall the states that border on Idaho when you're in a state of panic or to remember the formula for the area of a cone when your stomach is tied up in squiggles. The physical discomforts caused by anxiety—restlessness, a quickened heart rate, nausea, sweaty palms, and headaches—all militate against concentrating on the test questions. Anxious students are easily distracted and develop mental blocks that prevent them from doing as well as they could on standardized tests.

It's important to acknowledge your child's fears and worries, especially before an exam. Encourage her to think about why she becomes overwhelmed at the prospect of taking a test and to recognize how some thoughts are negative and self-defeating. Self-awareness is the first step in alleviating anxiety.

You might also show your child basic relaxation techniques to use during the exam. These maneuvers are not obscure or weird—you're not suggesting that she sit in a lotus position and repeat a mantra for 20 minutes. Simple activities go a long way: taking a few breaths, closing one's eyes for a half minute and thinking positive thoughts, tightening one's lips and then releasing them, stretching one's legs. Your child will notice how these easy movements can calm her and "unblock" her thinking.

The Overachiever

"I never had a problem getting Colleen to study. If anything, my concern is getting her to take it easy. It's so important to her that she receive on A on every paper, that she have the best grade in the class on every test." The challenge with overachieving children is not to enhance their expectations but to bring them down to realistic proportions. Colleen is a perfectionist; doing well on a test isn't good enough for her—nothing less than excellent will suffice.

Overachievers often have a streak of competitiveness, and while they may regularly get the best grades in their classes, they might not fare as well with standardized tests. Here the competition is comprised of hundreds of thousands, even millions of other students, and even most A students do not attain scores in the very top percentile. You need to make it clear to your child that she need not and should not expect to get the highest grade in the state—doing her best is perfectly acceptable.

The Underachiever

A parent laments his son's poor school record. "Alexander is really very bright though you'd never guess it from his grades. I already heard this from his teachers in the first grade. 'Alexander is a very smart kid,' they say, 'but he just doesn't live up to his potential.' And it's true. I don't know why, but he just doesn't work at his capacity. I wonder what's going to happen on these standardized tests."

Do You Need a Tutor?

◆

Should you hire a private tutor to help your child prepare for standardized tests?

As we've noted repeatedly, no one test in elementary or middle school carries that much weight. Later, in high school, it might make sense to have your child get professional help in preparing for a test such as the SAT, since acceptance to a college of your choice might ride on the results of this one test. The more important and larger question is whether a tutor can help your child with his general education. And the answer is: it depends.

Private tutors provide some obvious and genuine benefits. Competent test tutors are familiar with the design of standardized tests and can help children improve their scores. This isn't mere applesauce—becoming an accomplished test-taker is an extremely worthwhile skill for any student.

But tutors, we should caution, tend to be expensive, and there are alternatives. A plethora of self-study guides are available, both in printed form and as computer software. Their usefulness, however, depends on your child's diligence—and your own. It's a commonplace scenario: parents purchase a learning program only to have it compete for the dust with last year's new exercise machine.

In general, then, our suggestion is that in younger grades a private tutor for standardized tests is usually not necessary. On the other hand, if you seek tutoring help as part of a broader educational program, then it makes sense to include working with standardized tests as part of this larger effort.

The concern is legitimate. As with most of their school work, underachievers are also likely to dismiss the importance of doing well on standardized tests. This attitude becomes a self-fulfilling prophecy, and the student does, in fact, do poorly on his school work and on these tests.

> ◆
>
> *Children become adults when they realize they have a right not only to be right, but also to be wrong.*
> *—Thomas S. Szasz*
>
> ◆

Underachievement is the result of many possible causes, and we won't presume to tell you which is the culprit in your child's particular case. Here, however, are a few of the more common reasons for student underachievement.

Some children prefer to take it easy and receive just average grades. They thereby keep expectations about their work to a minimum and avoid the stress that accompanies having to do well.

For some children, high achievement comes at too high a cost. They have to work very hard to excel and the risk of failure is always a pressing threat. Too much is expected, so they react by lowering their standards and refuse to push themselves any harder.

And then there's boredom. Bright children sometimes lack motivation because the school material doesn't interest them. This boredom may take the form of inattentiveness, withdrawal, and turning in incomplete assignments.

Here are some things you can do to help your underachieving child:

◆ Recognize and encourage your child's attempts, not just their successes.

◆ Encourage him to evaluate his work before turning it in for a grade.

◆ Foster a shift in attitude from "I can't" to "I believe I can!"

◆ Provide remedial opportunities if needed. This gives the child an opportunity to excel in an environment where mistakes are an acceptable part of the learning process.

◆ Begin test preparation with easier tests to build confidence and momentum. Slowly move up to more challenging work.

But beware: don't place a permanent label of underachiever on your child. This can become self-perpetuating. Rather, focus on his positive efforts while working on improving those "underachieving" subjects.

Problems with Time Management

He's the one in the family who's always late. Its time to leave for church and he's upstairs looking for his shoes. It's time for dinner and he's outside playing ball. He's late with his daily homework and waits for the night before the deadline to do the research paper assigned three weeks before.

Time management is a problem for many adults as well as young students. Teaching your child to appreciate the flow of time may help him avoid future decades of trouble. More immediately, you will help your child develop an essential skill for performing well on standardized tests.

Standardized tests are given under specified time constraints. The test designers expect that some children will not be able to finish in the time allocated. While some children can't complete the questions because the material is too difficult for them, others falter because they have failed to budget their time intelligently. A typical example of this misallocation is expending a huge chunk of time answering a single math problem, leaving little time to answer the remaining questions. The student may answer that one question correctly, but he's bound to answer all the other questions incorrectly.

Begin working with time budget skills at home. Assist your child in setting up a realistic daily schedule, making sure that he "builds in time" to allow for delays, extra work, and surprises.

When working on practice exams, pay particular attention to how time is distributed. Show your child how to mark the passage of minutes and to make shrewd guesses about how much time a particular section will take to complete. Make sure, too, that your child becomes comfortable abandoning intractable questions so that he can turn his attention to the next questions on the test.

Chapter 3

◆

Standardized Tests: An Essential Score Card

S tates, school districts, and even individual schools all get involved in the selection of standardized tests. The tests typically are chosen from among a large array published by commercial testing companies. The selection process, as you might expect, is often guided as much by economic and political factors as by educational needs. And the decisions about which and how many tests to use varies considerably from state to state.

For example, in 1997-1998, Idaho and Arizona used just one statewide test, while other states—Rhode Island and Florida among them—had their students take several tests. In addition, states are increasingly developing their own assessment instruments, either "in-house" or through contracts with commercial publishers.

That's the states. Some school districts also decide to administer their own selection of standardized tests and contract directly with commercial test publishers. These tests are given in addition to the state-mandated exams.

When it comes to standardized tests, therefore, there is no standard procedure for choosing tests. In any given year, your child may take several tests, each prepared by a different company, including a test developed by your own state department of education. And each of these tests may differ significantly from the others.

As you can imagine, this can become very confusing for the school, for teachers, and certainly for you, the parent. To gain a perspective on this kaleidoscope of standardized tests, you could use a succinct, descriptive summary of the various assessment tools currently marketed in this country. Here is that overview.

NORM-REFERENCED TESTS

The following tests fall into the *norm-referenced* test category because test scores are reported as percentile ratings. You'll recall that the percentile figure reflects a comparison of a student's performance with that of the "norm," or average student at the particular grade level. For example, an 8th grade student who performs at the 87th percentile on the Iowa Test of Basic Skills mathematics test has performed better than 87% of the norming group, the statistically designed set of students representing all U.S. 8th graders. This, by the way, is a very good score.

Iowa Test of Basic Skills (ITBS)
Developed/published by: Houghton Mifflin/Riverside Publishing
Stated purpose: To provide a thorough assessment of student performance in basic skills. The full ITBS battery includes tests of reading, language arts, mathematics, social studies, science, and information sources.
Norm group: The current ITBS norm group was obtained through a national administration of the ITBS in Spring 1995.
Description: The ITBS is part of Houghton Mifflin's Iowa Tests series, which is comprised of three assessment products. The

two other components are the Iowa Test of Educational Development (ITED) and the Test of Achievement and Proficiency (TAP), both of which are designed for assessing students in grades 9-12.

The Iowa Tests measure a variety of skills and content areas that are considered essential to any child's education. As with most major test publishers, Houghton Mifflin/Riverside provides comprehensive test scoring and customization options and offers a variety of open-ended, performance assessment, and ability tests that can be combined with the ITBS to create what the company calls an "integrated and multi-dimensional assessment instrument."

States that use the ITBS in their statewide assessment program: Georgia, Idaho, Mississippi, Oklahoma, Washington

Metropolitan Achievement Test (MAT)

Developed/published by: Harcourt Brace Educational Measurement

Stated purpose: To provide a standardized assessment instrument that "reflects today's emphasis on the assessment of critical thinking in a realistic context."

Norm group: A full range of norm groups, based on national samples of students.

Description: The Metropolitan Achievement Test contains assessment components that measure student achievement in five disciplines: reading, mathematics, science, language, and social studies. The test is designed to measure content mastery/knowledge in terms of achievement, as well as thinking and reasoning skills. The MAT focuses on process as well as factual knowledge and features multiple-choice questions that require students to perform tasks and process information.

States that use the MAT in their statewide assessment program: Rhode Island, South Carolina

Stanford Achievement Test (SAT)

Developed/published by: Harcourt Brace Educational Measurement

Stated purpose: To provide teachers, schools, school districts, and states with a flexible assessment tool that yields comprehensive information about student performance.

Norm group: A large national sample of students in grades K-12 as well as other norm groups from Catholic schools, independent/private schools, schools in districts designated as high socio-economic status, and schools in urban/metropolitan areas.

Description: The Stanford Achievement Test, currently in its 9th series, should not to be confused with the *other* SAT—the Scholastic Assessment Test taken by all college-bound students. This test is a modular battery of exams that combines traditional norm-referenced testing with a cognitive ability test (the Otis-Lennon School Ability Test), performance assessments, and criterion-referenced test modules. States, districts, and schools can purchase any one of several SAT test batteries or choose a customized package of tests that meets their specific needs.

According to Harcourt Brace, content and questions on the SAT are aligned with most current national content standards projects, including, for example, the National Council of Teachers of Mathematics curriculum standards and the American Association for the Advancement of Science Project 2061 "Benchmarks for Scientific Literacy." Harcourt Brace publishes a variety of SAT-related support materials for parents and teachers.

States that use the SAT in their statewide assessment program: Alabama, Arizona, Arkansas, California, District of Columbia, Utah, Virginia

TerraNova/Comprehensive Test of Basic Skills (CTBS)
Developed/published by: CTB/McGraw-Hill

Stated purpose: To provide a standardized assessment instrument for teachers to then help their students attain their academic goals.

Norm group: A large national sample of students in grades K-12, stratified by geographic region, community type, district size, and socio-economic status.

Description: TerraNova comprises a series of assessments for grades K-12, including the "new" version of the California Test of Basic Skills, CTB/McGraw-Hill's long-standing norm-referenced K-12 assessment product. TerraNova test modules, available for grades K-12, test mathematics, science, social studies, and reading/language arts. Supplementary tests include word analysis, vocabulary, language mechanics, spelling, and mathematics computation.

States that use TerraNova in their statewide assessment program: Tennessee, Wisconsin

CTP III

Developed/published by: Educational Records Bureau (ERB)

Stated purpose: To measure achievement in grades 1-12 and verbal and quantitative ability in grades 3-12 and to differentiate among the ". . . most able students (those who typically rank above the 80th percentile on other standardized tests)."

Norm group: In addition to national and local norms, ERB provides annually updated independent and suburban school norms.

Description: The CTP III is a norm-referenced test aimed at the independent and suburban school market. Features include: mathematics and quantitative ability tests that are consistent with current National Council of Teachers of Mathematics standards; varying response formats targeted for different ability levels (e.g., students below grade 4 mark their answers right in the test booklet rather than on separate scoring sheets); and the ability to create standard score reports normed for students who take the test under non-standard conditions because of physical limitations.

The CTP III emphasizes questions that "tap higher-order thinking skills" and process-related questions, in addition to traditional content-related questions.

States that use the CTP III in their statewide assessment program: None as of this printing

CRITERION-REFERENCED TESTS

In *criterion-referenced* tests, you'll remember, a student's performance is measured against a standard—not, as with norm-referenced tests, against an average. Test administrators establish a set of expectations—for example, of what eighth graders should know about science—and design a test to determine whether, in fact, students are achieving this level of learning. The leading criterion-referenced tests are described in the following section.

Degrees of Reading Power (DRP)

Developed/published by: Touchstone Applied Science Associates (TASA)

Stated purpose: To measure how well students understand the meaning of written text in "real-life situations." Because the DRP is designed to provide a broad picture of individual student achievement and skill level, the company maintains that test results can be used to support a variety of educational objectives. Among these are the ability to select appropriate instructional materials, inform parents about their child's performance, allocate resources to school districts, document school accountability, set and maintain promotion standards, determine eligibility for graduation, place students into adult basic education and GED programs of study, and evaluate student progress in adult literacy programs.

Norm group: Although the DRP is a criterion-referenced test, TASA can provide norm-referenced scores that compare individual student performance with that of a national sample of students.

Description: According to TASA, DRP tests are ". . . single-objective tests that measure how well students understand the surface meaning of what they read. As such, they measure the process of reading rather than products of reading such as main idea and author purpose."

The DRP is available at all grade levels (1-12) and can be used to measure achievement in a given year as well as to track student progress from year to year. Because the DRP is an untimed test, the company points out that slow readers are not penalized or subject to undue stress.

New Standards Reference Examinations

Developed/published by: The National Center on Education and the Economy/The Learning and Development Center of the University of Pittsburgh/Harcourt Brace Educational Publishing

Stated purpose: New Standards tests are ". . . referenced to the New Standards Performance Standards in order to gauge student progress toward meeting those standards." States that implement the New Standards Assessment Program receive materials that define the specific content areas that the New Standards project expects students to know at specified grade levels. Also provided are "work samples" and "commentaries," which provide additional details about the scope and type of knowledge included in each content area.

Description: The New Standards project is a prime example of a standards-based performance and school improvement strategy. The project currently focuses on four subject areas: English/language arts, mathematics, science, and applied learning.

The New Standards Reference Examinations are based on content standards developed by professional and educational organizations and include the science benchmarks developed by the American Association for Advancement of Science Project 2061 and the National Research Council as well as the mathematics content standards developed by the National Council of Teachers of Mathematics.

New Standards examinations are available at elementary and middle school (as well as high school) levels, and have been extensively field tested.

States that use New Standards testing products in their statewide assessment program: Rhode Island

ABILITY AND APTITUDE TESTS

Unlike norm-referenced tests, which measure a child's achievement by comparing his performance on a test with that of a "norm group" of students at the same academic level, or criterion-referenced tests, which measure how well a student has mastered a given subject area, aptitude tests measure something more personal: a student's cognitive ability.

What is cognitive ability? *Cognition* describes the process of learning and understanding—cognitive ability, then, as assessed by standardized testing instruments, describes the level at which a child is capable of absorbing and using new concepts. These tests, in other words, measure potential achievement rather than the mastery of actual facts.

The answer must lie in learning better ways of learning.
—Marvin Minsky

While many students who score high on cognitive ability tests also perform well in the classroom and on norm- and criterion-referenced tests, some children with high aptitudes do not do well in these other contexts. Conversely, a student may perform at only an average level in cognitive tests yet do well in school and on other kinds of exams.

Cognitive ability tests, therefore, can be useful to parents and teachers because the results may highlight discrepancies and exhibit areas that require attention. For example, a child who scores high on a test of cognitive ability but is only mediocre in class has the potential to do better—why isn't he? Find out: perhaps the child is bored in class, or has an undiagnosed learning disability. Some schools look for such discrepancies themselves and administer a test of cognitive ability along with norm and general tests.

Often, schools that administer norm-referenced tests also administer a companion test of cognitive ability. Two examples of commercially published pairs of achievement and cognitive ability tests are the Iowa Test of Basic Skills (norm-referenced achievement) and the Cognitive Abilities Test (CogAT)—both from Houghton Mifflin/Riverside Publishing—and the Stanford Achievement Test (norm-referenced achievement) and the Otis-Lennon School Ability Test (OLSAT)—both from Harcourt Brace Educational Measurement. Through a comparison of the results of linked tests, a meaningful profile of the child's educational progress emerges.

Following are brief descriptions of the most popular tests of cognitive ability.

Cognitive Abilities Test (CogAT)

Developed/published by: Houghton Mifflin/Riverside Publishing

Stated purpose: To "assess students' abilities in reasoning and problem solving using verbal, quantitative, and spatial (non-verbal) symbols." The CogAT is intended to be administered in conjunction with the Iowa Test of Basic Skills (ITBS) to provide schools, teachers, and parents with additional information about a student's developmental abilities and potential.

Norm group: The CogAT is concurrently normed with the three tests in the Iowa Tests series: the Iowa Test of Basic Skills (grades K-8), the Tests of Achievement and Proficiency (TAP), and the Iowa Tests of Educational Development (ITED).

Description: The CogAT is designed to assess student cognitive development levels. When combined with the ITBS, it provides teachers and parents with a picture of a student's achievement as well as his ability. For example, a fourth grade student might take the ITBS in April of the school year (level 4.8) and achieve a reading score level of 4.2, indicating that she is slightly below grade level. At the same time, the student might also take the CogAT—with results from the verbal section indicating a much higher cognitive ability. These two tests, taken in conjunction, provide teacher and parent with information they need to design an educational program to help this student perform up to her cognitive ability.

Otis-Lennon School Ability Test (OLSAT)

Developed/published by: Harcourt Brace Educational Measurement

Stated purpose: The OLSAT assesses reasoning and complex thinking skills. Test results can be used to identify a student's relative strengths and weaknesses and help create individual educational plans. When administered as a companion of the Stanford Achievement Test, a "…meaningful comparison of ability and school achievement is obtained."

Norm group: Current versions of the OLSAT have been normed in conjunction with the four major Harcourt Brace Educational Measurement assessments currently in use: the Stanford Achievement Test Series 8th and 9th editions and the Metropolitan Achievement Test 6th and 7th editions.

Description: The OLSAT, according to Harcourt Brace, is designed to measure "…the cognitive abilities that relate to a student's ability to learn and succeed in school."

NATIONAL STANDARDIZED TESTS

The following two tests—the National Assessment of Educational Progress (NAEP) and the Third International Mathematics and Science Study (TIMSS)—are national tests that are annually or periodically administered to statistically significant student samples in each state that participates in the testing program. The aim is to gain statistical information about the level of American student achievement. Therefore, the scores are reported only in aggregate form and only measure overall, not individual, educational achievement and progress. The state doesn't get the individual scores, the districts don't, the schools don't, nor do the parents.

These general scores, however, receive wide public attention. For instance, in January 1998, the results of the TIMSS was a major news story. In addition to students in this country, the test was administered to similar groups of students from more than 40 other countries, and the results indicated that U.S. students are far behind comparable student populations in most of the nations participating in this test. Note, again, that this is a general result that tells us nothing about the individual performance of Joe Anybody in Streetsmart, Tennessee.

The Voluntary National Test Program

◆

President Clinton's Voluntary National Test Program continues to draw both intense support and opposition in the Congress and among citizens at large. The heart of this controversy is the establishment of the national standards that these tests are designed to assess. Some legislators view national standards as an encroachment on the authority of the states and local districts, while others see standards as a unifying and vital step toward improved education for all children.

Despite this debate, the development of national standardized tests continues full steam ahead. In November 1997, Congress authorized the National Assessment Governing Board to develop national standardized tests. The Board has established a five-year plan for implementing these tests throughout the country. In the meantime, states and local school districts continue to administer standardized tests that cover new subject areas and in greater depth than ever before. While full deployment of national tests is still on the horizon, standardized tests are already an integral part of every American child's education.

TIMSS (Third International Mathematics and Science Study)

TIMSS is the largest and most comprehensive international comparison of science and mathematics education ever conducted. In 1997, more than 500,000 students in 41 countries were tested. The study focuses on children aged 9, 13, and in the last year of high school. In the United States, this means that 4th, 8th, and 12th grade students are tested.

TIMSS is based on the premise that curriculum and teaching methods help determine what children learn. To this end, the 1996 TIMSS was designed to analyze curriculum—to uncover the relationship between what is taught (curriculum) and how it is taught (teaching methods) and what students learn. The 1997 TIMSS was designed to assess student achievement levels.

The educators, researchers, and scientists who administer TIMSS in the United States (the U.S. TIMSS research center is housed at Michigan State University) view the test as an important source of information on how effectively current science and mathematics curricula are educating U.S. students. These exams also provide a valuable incentive for reform of the science and mathematics education in the country.

It is unlikely that your child will take the TIMSS since it is only given to sample groups of students in participating states. Nonetheless, these tests have an increasingly important impact on what your child will study in science and math in the years ahead.

National Assessment of Educational Progress (NAEP)

NAEP, now in its 28th year, is a nationally administered assessment program designed to measure the educational accomplishments and progress of U.S. students in selected subject areas at the 4th, 8th, and 12th grade level. The NAEP program is mandated by Congress with the stated purpose of providing U.S. educators and policymakers with reliable, relevant, and useful information about the skills of U.S. students each year. The data is published annually by the U.S. Department of Education's Public Affairs Office and is available to the public.

The subjects assessed by the NAEP include civics/citizenship, mathematics, science, music, writing, geography, U.S. history, and reading. Subjects are tested on a rotating basis, with some subjects (e.g., reading) tested more frequently than others. This enables the NCES to track scores at a given grade level over time—on the basis of these scores, for example, they can compare the reading ability of 4th graders in 1984 with the reading levels of 4th graders in 1998.

The NAEP is directed by the Commissioner of Education Statistics, at the U.S. Department of Education's National Center for

Education Statistics (NCES). The program is governed by the National Assessment Governing Board (NAGB), which is appointed by the Secretary of Education. Each year, NAGB members decide which subject areas will be tested and which data will be reported.

Again, the odds are that your child will not take an NAEP test since it is only given to a sample number of students across the country. But this test, too, is already influencing the curricula in your child's school and will have an even greater influence in the future.

Standardized Tests, State by State

◆

A Parent's Guide to What's Tested When

ALABAMA

Test: Stanford Achievement Test (SAT), 9th Edition

ALASKA

Test: California Achievement Test (CAT), 5th Edition
Grade level: 4, 8, 11

ARIZONA

Test: Stanford Achievement Test (SAT), 9th Edition

ARKANSAS

Test: Stanford Achievement Test (SAT), 9th Edition, Complete Battery
Subjects tested: Math, reading/language arts, social studies, science
Grade level: 5, 7, 10

Test: Criterion-referenced test
Subjects tested: Math, English, reading, writing
Grade level: 4, 8, 11, 12

CALIFORNIA

Test: Stanford Achievement Test (SAT), 9th Edition
Subjects tested: Reading/language arts, math
Grade level: 2, 3, 4, 5, 6, 7, 8

Test: Statewide standards-based assessment being developed

COLORADO

Test: Colorado Student Assessment Program (CSAP) developed in-state to match statewide curriculum frameworks

CONNECTICUT

Test: Connecticut Mastery Test (state developed)
Grade level: 4, 6, 8

DELAWARE

Test: Delaware State Testing Program (DSTP)—standards based, developed in-state
Subjects tested: English/language arts, math
Grade level: 3, 5, 8, 10
Subjects tested: Science, social studies (starting in 1999)
Grade level: 4, 6, 8, 11

DISTRICT OF COLUMBIA

Test: Stanford Achievement Test (SAT), 9th Edition
Subjects tested: Math, reading
Grade level: 1, 2, 3, 4, 5, 6, 7, 8, 9, 10, 11

FLORIDA

Test: Florida Comprehensive Achievement Test (FCAT)—developed for Florida by CTB/McGraw Hill to reflect state curriculum standards

Test: Each district chooses its own norm-referenced test; tests in use include California Achievement Test, Stanford Achievement Test, National Achievement Test, Iowa Test of Basic Skills, others

GEORGIA

Test: Georgia Kindergarten Assessment Program (GKAP)—state developed
Grade level: Rising kindergarten students

Test: Iowa Test of Basic Skills (ITBS)
Subjects tested: Reading, math
Grade level: 3, 5, 8

HAWAII

Test: Statewide assessment system under development for year 2000
Grade level: 3, 6, 8

IDAHO

Test: Iowa Test of Basic Skills (ITBS)

ILLINOIS

Test: Illinois Goal Assessment Program (IGAP)
Subjects tested: Reading, math, writing
Grade level: 3, 6, 8, 10
Subjects tested: Science, social science
Grade level: 4, 7, 11

INDIANA

Test: Indiana Statewide Testing for Educational Progress (ISTEP) developed to meet Indiana State standards by CTB/McGraw Hill
Subjects tested: Reading/language arts, math
Grade level: 3, 6, 8, 10

IOWA

Test: Iowa does not currently have a statewide assessment program

KANSAS

Test: State-developed assessment tests, standards based
Subjects tested: Reading
Grade level: 3, 7, 10
Subjects tested: Writing, science
Grade level: 5, 8, 10
Subjects tested: Math
Grade level: 4, 7, 10

Subjects tested: Social studies
Grade level: 5, 8, 11

KENTUCKY

Test: Kentucky Instructional Results Information System (KIRIS)
Subjects tested: Science, social studies, math, reading, arts/humanities, practical living/vocational studies
Grade level: 4, 8, 11

LOUISIANA

Test: California Achievement Test
Subjects tested: Reading/language arts, math
Grade level: 4

Test: Louisiana Educational Assessment Program (LEAP)
Subjects tested: Language arts, math
Grade level: 3

Test: Statewide standards-based assessment program being developed

MAINE

Test: Maine Educational Assessment
Subjects tested: Reading, writing, math, science, social studies, arts and humanities
Grade level: 4, 8, 11
Subjects tested: Health
Grade level: 4,8

MARYLAND

Test: Maryland School Performance Assessment Program (MSPAP)
Subjects tested: Reading, math, English/language arts, science, social studies
Grade level: 3, 5, 8, 11

MASSACHUSETTS

Test: Massachusetts Educational Assessment Program
Subjects tested: English/language arts, math, science/technology; history and social science starting in 1999
Grade level: 4, 8, 10

MICHIGAN

Test: Michigan Educational Assessment Program (MEAP)
Subjects tested: Math, reading
Grade level: 4, 7
Subjects tested: Science, writing
Grade level: 5, 8

MINNESOTA

Test: Minnesota Comprehensive Assessment Program
Subjects tested: Reading, math
Grade level: 3, 5, 8-12
Subjects tested: Writing
Grade level: 5

MISSISSIPPI

Test: Iowa Test of Basic Skills (ITBS)
Subjects tested: Reading/language arts, math
Grade level: 4, 5, 6, 7, 8, 9

Test: Iowa Test of Basic Skills/Iowa Test of Achievement and Proficiency (combined)
Grade level: 9

MISSOURI

Test: Missouri Assessment Program (MAP)—replaces the Missouri Mastery and Achievement Test program; MAP is being developed by the state in conjunction with CTB/McGraw Hill
Subjects tested: Math
Grade level: 4, 8, 10
Subjects tested: English (starting in 1999)
Grade level: 3, 7, 11

Subjects tested: Science (starting in 1999)
Grade level: 3, 7, 10
Subjects tested: Social studies (starting in 2000)
Grade level: 4, 8, 11

MONTANA

Test: Districts can choose from among commercially prepared tests
Subjects tested: Math, reading, other "core subjects"
Grade level: 4, 8, 10

NEBRASKA

Test: Nebraska does not currently have a statewide assessment program

NEVADA

Test: Districts can choose from among commercially prepared tests
Subjects tested: Reading, writing, math
Grade level: 4, 8, 11

NEW HAMPSHIRE

Test: New Hampshire Educational Improvement and Assessment Program (NHEIAP)
Subjects tested: English/language arts, math
Grade level: 3
Subjects tested: English/language arts, math, science, social studies
Grade level: 6, 10

NEW JERSEY

Test: Elementary School Proficiency Test (ESPA)
Grade level: 4

NEW YORK

Test: Pupil Evaluation Program (PEP)
Subjects tested: Reading, math
Grade level: 3, 6
Subjects tested: Writing
Grade level: 5

Test: Program Evaluation Test (PET)
Subjects tested: Science
Grade level: 4
Subjects tested: Social studies
Grade level: 6, 8

Test: New standards-based tests are in development

NORTH CAROLINA

Test: North Carolina End of Grade Test
Subjects tested: Reading, math
Grade level: 3–8

Test: North Carolina Developed Open-Ended Written (essay) Test
Subjects tested: Reading, math
Grade level: 4, 8

NORTH DAKOTA

Tests: CTBS, Fifth Edition: Terra Nova, *and companion test:* Test of
    Cognitive Skills, 2nd Edition
Subjects tested: Multi-Subject Battery Test
Grade level: 4, 6, 8,10

OHIO

Test: Ohio Proficiency Test
Subjects tested: Reading, writing, math, science, citizenship
Grade level: 4, 6, 9, 12

OKLAHOMA

Test: Iowa Test of Basic Skills
Grade level: 3, 7

Test: Oklahoma Core Curriculum Tests
Subjects tested: Math, science, reading, history, writing
Grade level: 5, 8, 11

OREGON

Test: State-developed criterion-referenced tests
Subjects tested: Writing
Grade level: 5, 8, 10
Subjects tested: Reading and literature, math
Grade level: 3, 5, 8, 10

PENNSYLVANIA

Test: Pennsylvania System of School Assessment (state developed)
Subjects tested: Reading
Grade level: 5, 8, 11
Subjects tested: Writing
Grade level: 6, 9
Subjects tested: Math
Grade level: 5, 8, 11

RHODE ISLAND

Test: Metropolitan Achievement Test
Grade level: 4, 8

Test: Rhode Island Writing Test (state developed)
Grade level: 3, 7, 10

Test: New Standards
Subjects tested: Math
Grade level: 4, 8, 10
Subjects tested: English/language arts
Grade level: 4, 8

Test: Health Education Assessment
Grade level: 5, 9

SOUTH CAROLINA

Test: South Carolina Basic Skills Assessment Program (BSAP)
Grade level: 3, 6, 8, 10

Test: Metropolitan Achievement Test, Seventh Edition (MAT7)
Subjects tested: Math, language arts
Grade level: 4, 5, 7, 9, 11

SOUTH DAKOTA

Test: Nationally standardized norm-referenced achievement and ability test
Subjects tested: Reading, math
Grade level: 2, 4, 8, 11
Subjects tested: Writing achievement
Grade level: 5, 9

TENNESSEE

Test: TerraNova, Complete Battery Plus
Subjects tested: Reading/language arts, math, science, social studies
Grade level: 3, 4, 5, 6, 7, 8

TEXAS

Test: Texas Assessment of Academic Skills (TAAS)
Subjects tested: Reading, math
Grade level: 3, 4, 5, 6, 7, 8, 10
Subjects tested: Writing
Grade level: 4, 8
Subjects tested: Social studies, science
Grade level: 8

UTAH

Test: Stanford Achievement Test (SAT), 9th Edition
Grade level: 5, 8, 11

VERMONT

Test: Vermont Comprehensive Assessment System (VCAS)
Subjects tested: Early reading
Grade level: 2
Subjects tested: Math, English/language arts
Grade level: 4, 8, 10
Subjects tested: Science
Grade level: 6, 11
Subjects tested: History, social studies, geography
Grade level: 6, 9, 11

Test: Local districts choose a norm-referenced test (not mandatory)
Grade level: 5, 9, 11

VIRGINIA

Test: Stanford Achievement Test (SAT), 9th Edition, Form TA
Subjects tested: Reading/language arts, math (science and social studies optional)
Grade level: 4, 6, 9

Test: Virginia Standards of Learning (SOL) Test (state developed)
Subjects tested: English, math, science, social studies
Grade level: 3
Subjects tested: English, math, science, social studies, computer technology
Grade level: 5
Subjects tested: English, math, science, social studies, computer technology
Grade level: 8

WASHINGTON

Test: Comprehensive Test of Basic Skills
Subjects tested: Reading/language arts, math
Grade level: 4, 8, 11

Test: Standards-based assessments are being developed

WEST VIRGINIA

Test: Metropolitan Readiness Test
Grade level: Kindergarten

Test: Statewide Assessment Program tests
Subjects tested: Reading, math, language, listening
Grade level: 1, 2
Subjects tested: Listening
Grade level: 3, 4, 5, 6, 7, 8
Subjects tested: Reading/language arts, spelling, math, science, social sciences
Grade level: 3, 4, 5, 6, 7, 8, 9, 10, 11

WISCONSIN

Test: TerraNova
Grade level: 4, 8, 10

Test: Wisconsin Reading Comprehension Test
Grade level: 3

Chapter 4

Sample Questions from Popular Standardized Tests

I t's time to roll up your sleeves and get to work.

Thus far, we've been discussing what tests are designed to accomplish and how they've become an integral part of our educational landscape. We've also noted some general strategies parents can adopt to improve their children's scores.

Now it's time to get specific. We need to look at the tests themselves so that your child will have a clear idea of what he can expect and what learning skills need special attention.

This chapter contains sample questions from three of the most widely used standardized tests: the Iowa Test of Basic Skills (Houghton Mifflin/Riverside Publishing), the Stanford Achievement Test (Harcourt Brace), and the TerraNova (CTB/McGraw Hill). These representative questions were selected to give you an overview of the range of formats, test styles, and subject areas that appear in standardized tests. Although the test items presented in this chapter were provided by test publishers, they are not, for obvious reasons, actual questions that are used on current tests. But no matter: they are exactly like the questions that your child will encounter on the real tests.

We should reiterate, however, that because of both internal industry competition and external political pressures—in addition to new developments in educational research—test publishers constantly revise their products.

We noted earlier that there is no standard for standardized tests. Even though different standardized tests may seek to measure the same student ability or achievement, each proceeds from its own educational philosophy and has its own distinct format and style. As you review the test items presented here, you'll observe, for example, how the approach of the Iowa Test of Basic Skills differs from that of the TerraNova.

Your child's standardized tests will, of course, get harder as she gets older. The reading comprehension passages are longer and require more complex editing and grammar/usage questions. She will be expected to perform more difficult arithmetical computations and have familiarity with more advanced mathematical concepts.

It's not just the questions that are more complex, however, but also the testing procedure. For example, younger children mark their answers right in the test booklet, circling the correct picture, word, or number, and because the answers are graded by hand, some sloppiness is allowed. The machine-tallied answers in multiple-choice tests given to older children, on the other hand, require neat entries. Be on the lookout for any difficulty your children may have making this transition.

Okay. Let's get started. We've sorted the test questions into four general topic areas:

◆ Mathematics
◆ Science
◆ Social Studies
◆ Reading/English/Language Arts

Each topic area presents increasingly harder questions designed for older children.

The test questions under the heading *Iowa Tests of Basic Skills* are reprinted with permission from Riverside Publishing. Copyright © 1996 by The University of Iowa. All rights reserved. No part of this work may be reproduced or transmitted in any form or by any means, electronic or mechanical, including photocopying and recording, or by any information storage or retrieval system without the prior written permissions of The Riverside Publishing Company unless such copying is expressly permitted by federal copyright law. Address inquiries to Permissions, The Riverside Publishing Company, 425 Spring Lake Drive, Itasca, Illinois 60143-2079.

Test questions under the heading *Stanford Achievement Tests* are from the Guides for Classroom Planning of the Stanford Achievement Test: Ninth Edition. Copyright © 1996 by Harcourt Brace & Company. Reproduced by permission. All rights reserved.

Test questions under the heading *TerraNova* are reprinted with permission from The McGraw-Hill Companies, Inc. Questions are taken from *TerraNova Sample Pages: A Look Inside,* copyright © 1998 by CTB/McGraw-Hill. *TerraNova®* is a registered trademark of The McGraw-Hill Companies, Inc.

MATHEMATICS

If you haven't looked at a math test for a couple of decades, you're in for a surprise. We've come a long way from the days when mathematical ability was tested through endless addition and subtraction problems and mind-numbing assignments asking you to "fill in the missing number"—"What," you wondered, "does any of this have to do with the real world?" Somebody must have been listening.

Today's standardized tests measure mathematical skills and concepts that have direct application in everyday life. The questions test the student's mathematical ability by using scenarios and problems that emerge from ordinary, routine circumstances.

Representative math questions from standardized tests follow.

Computation/Number Skills

TerraNova

How many handprints are in the picture?

○   8
○   9
○   10
○   11

The correct answer is 10.

Which of these numbers is greater than 362?

A   359
B   381
C   352
D   360

The correct answer is B.

Abby is going to glue this drawing onto a posterboard. She wants the posterboard to extend 2 inches beyond the drawing on all four sides. What size should her posterboard be?

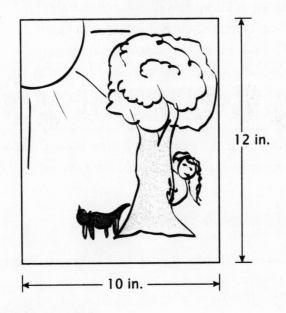

F   10 inches by 12 inches
G   12 inches by 14 inches
H   14 inches by 16 inches
J   18 inches by 20 inches

The correct answer is H.

At 3:00 P.M., it was 13°F. By 9:00 P.M., it was 28°F colder. What was the temperature at 9:00 P.M.?

A   15°F
B   –15°F
C   –28°F
D   –41°F

The correct answer is B.

Look at the table of interesting events in history.

Interesting Events in History

1748	Town of Pompeii is discovered in Italy.
1799	The Rosetta Stone is discovered in Egypt.
1824	Dinosaur bones are discovered in Europe.
1879	Prehistoric cave paintings are found in Spain.
1991	A six-thousand-year-old body is found in the Swiss Alps.

Use your ruler to make a number line to show the information in the table. You must make a consistent scale and label each point.

Iowa Test of Basic Skills

Which of these words does <u>not</u> tell how long something is?

A   Inch
B   Foot
C   Yard
D   Pound

The correct answer is D.

How much money is shown below?

J   36¢
K   44¢
L   54¢
M $3.24

The correct answer is K.

Which number sentence is true?

A   42 > 21
B   27 > 36
C   63 < 57
D   71 < 67

The correct answer is A.

Which number should be on the plain bead to complete the pattern?

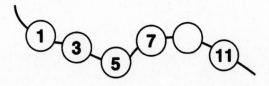

J   6
K   8
L   9
M   10

The correct answer is L.

Stanford Achievement Test, Primary 2

The next two questions are read aloud to students, who are asked to mark the correct answer in their test booklet.

What number would make this number sentence true?

14 – ☐ = 14

14   7   1   0
O   O   O   O

The correct answer is 0.

Stanford Achievement Test, Primary 3

Library Summer Reading

Name	Number of Pages Read
Maria	537
Pedro	542
Jean	65
Kim	489

Who read the most pages?

Ⓐ   Maria
Ⓑ   Pedro
Ⓒ   Jean
Ⓓ   Kim

The correct answer is B.

$7 \times 8 = \square$

54	56	58	63	NH
Ⓐ	Ⓑ	Ⓒ	Ⓓ	Ⓔ

The correct answer is B.

*The NH, or "Not Here," option is used carefully in Stanford 9. Any items that could possibly have another answer, such as an unreduced fraction, do not have the NH option.

Problem Solving

Iowa Test of Basic Skills

Mike and Beth were helping their father make meatballs. Mike made 12 meatballs and Beth made 9 meatballs. **How many meatballs did they make together?**

A   3
B   19
C   21
D   Not given

The correct answer is C.

Beth and Mike's mother said that about 16 meatballs can be made from 1 pound of hamburger. **How can Mike and Beth find out how many meatballs they can make from 2 pounds of hamburger?**

J   Multiply 16 by 2
K   Divide 16 by 2
L   Add 16 and 2
M   Subtract 2 from 16

The correct answer is J.

Stanford Achievement Test, Primary 2

I am inside of the circle and square, but not inside the triangle. What number am I?

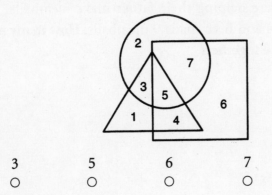

3	5	6	7
○	○	○	○

The correct answer is 7.

Stanford Achievement Test, Primary 3

Lucy paid $16.47 for a bird.

She gave the pet store clerk a $20 bill.

How much change should Lucy receive?

$36.47	$16.27	$4.47	$4.53	NH
Ⓐ	Ⓑ	Ⓒ	Ⓓ	Ⓔ

The correct answer is E.

Stanford Achievement Test, Intermediate

Which has the greatest perimeter?

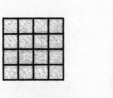

A

C

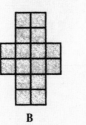

B

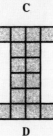

D

The correct answer is C.

If 2 of the numbered disks are switched, these subtraction problems will all have the same differences. Which 2 disks are they?

(56) (44)   (38) (40)
A   C

(40) (44)   (28) (22)
B   D

The correct answer is D.

Estimation

TerraNova

Jar 1 and Jar 2 are the same size and shape. There are 389 marbles in Jar 1. Which of these is the best estimate for the number of marbles in Jar 2?

A   200

B   400

C   600

D   800

The correct answer is D.

The Azteca Stadium in Mexico seats 107,000 people. According to the information in the article, about how many people attended the soccer series?

**Soccer Series
SOLD OUT!**

All 10 games of the soccer series at Aztec Stadium were completely sold out!

A   10,000

B   100,000

C   1,000,000

D   10,000,000

The correct answer is C.

Stanford Achievement Test, Intermediate

A radio station has $9000 to give away. Each week the station awards between $100 and $200. About how many weeks will it take for all of the money to be given away?

F   6

G   40

H   60

J   100

The correct answer is H.

Charts and Graphs

TerraNova

How many balls of yarn did she then have? *(This question is asked orally.)*

O   4

O   5

O   7

O   9

The correct answer is 5.

Stanford Achievement Test, Intermediate

Each  is 0.01.

What number is shown in this picture?

F   0.0357
G   0.357
H   3.57
J   35.7

The correct answer is H.

Pattern Recognition/Spatial Relationships

Iowa Test of Basic Skills

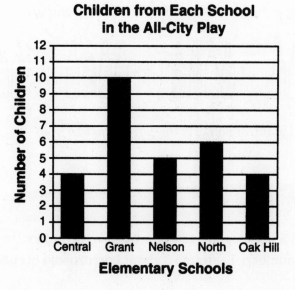

How many children from Nelson School were in the play?

A   4
B   5
C   6
D   10

The correct answer is B.

Which two schools had the same number of children in the play?

J   Nelson and Grant
K   Nelson and Oak Hill
L   Central and Nelson
M   Central and Oak Hill

The correct answer is M.

Decimals, Percentages, and Fractions

Stanford Achievement Test, Primary 2

Which group shows one-fourth of the bottles empty?

The second group of bottles is the correct answer.

TerraNova

Lorenzo is a beekeeper. Each year he sells the honey from his bee-hives. Do numbers 1 through 5 about Lorenzo and his bees.

1. Each hive has 1 queen bee, about 1,000 drones, and about 50,000 workers. About what percent of the bees in a hive are drones?

A   2%
B   5%
C   20%
D   50%

The correct answer is A.

2. The picture shows the dimensions of one of the frames that holds the honeycombs.

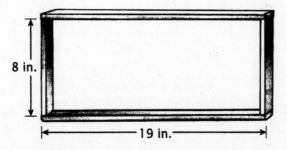

8 in.

19 in.

What length of board could Lorenzo cut into 4 pieces to make a frame?

F 27 inches
G 38 inches
H 54 inches
J 152 inches

The correct answer is H.

These are the prices Lorenzo charges for each size jar of honey. Use the information to help you do Numbers 3 through 5.

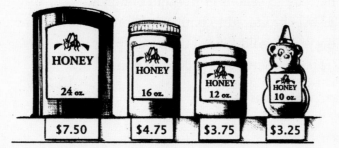

HONEY 24 oz.   HONEY 16 oz.   HONEY 12 oz.   HONEY 10 oz.

$7.50 $4.75 $3.75 $3.25

3. Which size jar costs the least per ounce?

A 24 oz.
B 16 oz.
C 12 oz.
D 10 oz.

The correct answer is B.

4. This year Lorenzo's bees produced 180 pounds of honey. If he sells all the honey in 12-ounce jars, how much money will he receive?

F $15
G $675
H $900
J $2160

The correct answer is H.

5. Look at the calculation Lorenzo made on his notepad. What did he find out?

A   There are 15 gallons in 1 pound of honey.
B   The bees produced 15 pounds of honey.
C   This year he sold 15% of the honey produced.
D   The bees produced 15 gallons of honey.

The correct answer is D.

Spatial Concepts and Geometry

Stanford Achievement Test, Primary 2

Look at the first shape. Which of these shapes has the same number of sides as the first shape?

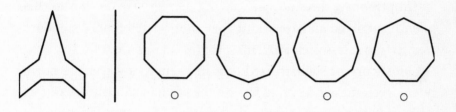

The second shape is correct.

Stanford Achievement Test, Primary 3

Nadine wants to fold her drawing in half so that both sides of the picture match exactly. Which is *not* a way she might fold it?

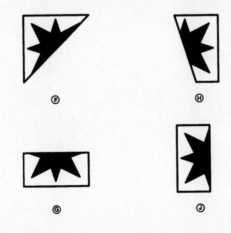

The correct answer is H.

SCIENCE

If Americans know anything about science, it's that they don't know enough. We continually read reports of how poorly American students fare on standardized science tests compared with students from other industrialized countries.

In response, the states are paying increased attention to their science curricula and are asking for criterion-referenced standardized tests to assess their students' progress in science.

Most current standardized tests in science, however, are norm-referenced and concentrate less on the student's inventory of facts than on her ability to "think scientifically." These tests seek to measure a child's understanding of basic scientific principles, her familiarity with the scientific method, and her ability to apply those principles and methods to everyday life. She will be asked to interpret data, explain scientific symbols, and design simple scientific experiments, including maps, tables, and graphs.

Sample science questions from norm-referenced tests follow.

Iowa Test of Basic Skills

Which animal probably would not be found in a forest habitat?

A   Fly
B   Frog
C   Beaver
D   Starfish

The correct answer is D.

Two balls are the same size, but the white ball floats in water and the green ball sinks. What does this observation tell us?

A   The green ball is heavier than the white ball.
B   The white ball has air in the middle of it.
C   White things float better than dark things.
D   Round things float better than square things.

The correct answer is A.

Stanford Achievement Test, Primary 2

Which graph shows that there are more animals than plants on Earth?

A   B   C

The correct answer is A.

The pictures in this row were taken at different times of the day. Which picture was taken when the sun was lowest in the sky?

○   ○   ○

The second picture is the correct answer.

Note that these questions are read to students verbally, and that students answer by marking the correct answer in the book.

At the River

Rivers are everywhere. Many people like to visit rivers. Answer the following questions about rivers and the things Kim does at the river. You should write enough so that other students could learn from your answers. You may use drawings with labels to help you explain your answers.

Kim and Rudy like to go to the river. The picture shows some of the things Kim saw along the river. Some of the things around the river are living and some are not living. Draw a circle around each thing in the picture that is living.

There is no one right answer; this open-ended question will be scored based on how many correct objects the child circles. Items that could be circled—because they are living things—include the raccoon, the plants, the birds, the lobster, and the trees.

Stanford Achievement Test, Primary 3

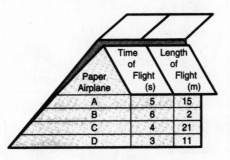

Paper Airplane	Time of Flight (s)	Length of Flight (m)
A	5	15
B	6	2
C	4	21
D	3	11

Which paper airplane flew the farthest?

A	B	C	D
Ⓕ	Ⓖ	Ⓗ	Ⓙ

The correct answer is H.

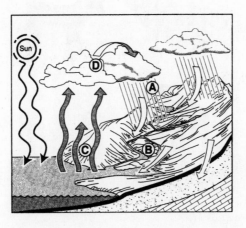

The diagram shows the water cycle. At which point in the cycle must water be changed from a liquid to a gas?

A	B	C	D
Ⓐ	Ⓑ	Ⓒ	Ⓓ

The correct answer is C.

Which animal has moved the most from Picture 1 to Picture 2?

The correct answer is H.

Which health habit is the most important to help keep people from getting sick?

Ⓐ   Brushing teeth after every meal
Ⓑ   Getting plenty of sleep
Ⓒ   Taking a daily bath
Ⓓ   Seeing a doctor twice a year

The correct answer is B.

Stanford Achievement Test, Intermediate

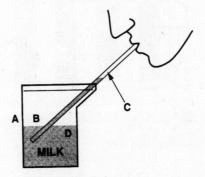

The picture shows a person drinking milk from a straw. In order for the milk to rise in the straw, where must air pressure be the lowest?

A   A

B   B

C   C

D   D

The correct answer is C.

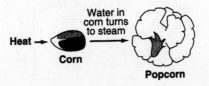

When the corn for popcorn is heated, water in the corn turns to steam and the corn pops. Why does steam cause the corn to pop?

F   Steam changes the molecules of the corn.

G   Steam takes up more space than water does.

H   Steam reacts with more substances in the corn than water does.

J   Steam is more cohesive than water.

The correct answer is G.

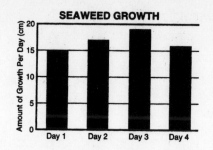

The graph shows the amount a seaweed grew each day. On which day did the seaweed grow the most?

F   1
G   2
H   3
J   4

The correct answer is H.

The picture shows different kinds of sunfish. Which of these is also a sunfish?

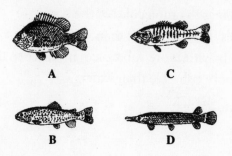

The correct answer is A.

TerraNova

The chart shows five groups that were used in an experiment to find out the best conditions for growing mold on bread. The experiment included a control group and four test groups. On the chart, you can see that each of the test groups has at least one thing that is different from the control group. The things that are different are called *variables.*

Conditions	Control Group	Test Group 1	Test Group 2	Test Group 3	Test Group 4
Light	off	on	off	off	on
Moisture	damp	damp	dry	damp	dry
Temperature	warm	warm	warm	hot	warm

Which test group has temperature as a variable?

A   Test Group 1
B   Test Group 2
C   Test Group 3
D   Test Group 4

The correct answer is C.

Potential energy is energy that is stored. This stored energy can be used later to do work. Which picture shows the greatest amount of potential energy stored in the weightlifter's barbells?

F   G   H   J

The correct answer is J.

SOCIAL STUDIES

As in the case of science, both educators and parents are disappointed in the level of knowledge of American students in the social sciences. Surveys repeatedly make explicit the woeful ignorance of history and geography among far too many of our youth. The impetus is growing, accordingly, for new standards in the social sciences and the design of criterion-referenced tests that will assess the implementation of these standards.

In the meantime, however, current standardized tests in the social sciences are predominantly norm-referenced and focus less on measuring the student's knowledge of facts than his understanding of grade-appropriate concepts and themes.

The subjects covered in these tests cover a wide swath, including U.S. history, government, and civic life; basic patterns of civilization (e.g., large human settlements tend to be near rivers); geography; and map reading and chart interpretation skills.

Representative social studies questions from current standardized tests follow.

Iowa Test of Basic Skills

Which tells what the symbols on a map mean?

A   The key
B   The grid
C   The scale
D   The compass rose

The correct answer is A.

Which of these did many European immigrants see when they first came to the United States?

A   B   C   D

The correct answer is D.

Stanford Achievement Test, Primary 2

Note that these questions are read to students verbally, and that students answer by marking the correct answer in the book.

Which president served in the 1800s? Was it President Washington, President Lincoln, or President Reagan?

The correct answer is the middle figure.

This timeline shows the invention of kinds of transportation. Where should the invention of the airplane go on the timeline? Is it closest to 1850, 1900, or 1950?

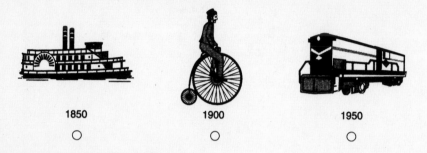

1850	1900	1950
○	○	○

The correct answer is 1900.

Which person works for a local government? Is it the house painter, the ballplayer, or the firefighter?

The correct answer is the firefighter.

Mr. Anderson has just been elected governor. Is he in charge of the country, a state, or a city?

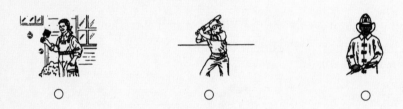

The correct answer is a state.

Stanford Achievement Test, Primary 3

According to the map key, which of these cities is the smallest?

Ⓕ   San Diego

Ⓖ   San Francisco

Ⓗ   Fresno

Ⓙ   Los Angeles

The correct answer is H.

Which state is shaded?

Ⓐ   Nevada

Ⓑ   Idaho

Ⓒ   Utah

Ⓓ   Arizona

The correct answer is A.

Producers are people who make sure there are things for people to buy. Producers supply two things—goods and services.

This list shows both types of producers. Add two more producers to each list.

Producers of Goods	Producers of Services
1. Miners	1. Doctors
2. Farmers	2. Sales People
3. Auto Workers	3. Airplane Pilots
4.	4.
5.	5.

How did you decide what to put in each list?

_____

_____

_____

_____

This question tests students' understanding of some basic principles of economics—and requires that they understand vocabulary words that have meaning and usage specific to this topic. There is a long list of acceptable answers for additional "producers of services" and "producers of goods"; the second part of the question, which asks students to explain why they answered as they did, is designed to make sure students understand—and can explain—why they made the choices they did.

Stanford Achievement Test, Intermediate

Which of these resulted from the American Revolution?

A   George III ordered all British soldiers to leave North America.
B   Many colonists who were loyal to the King moved to Canada.
C   Spain and France increased their attacks on the colonists.
D   George III was forced to leave the British throne.

The correct answer is B.

Areas with annual rainfall of more than 50 inches

Large evergreen forests

Moderate temperature ranges

Cool ocean currents from the north

Largest population centers along the coast

Which region of North America is the box referring to?

F   Gulf-Atlantic Coastal Plain
G   Appalachian Highlands
H   Arctic Coastal Plain
J   Pacific Mountains and Valleys

The correct answer is J.

The next two questions are presented to students orally; the teacher reads the passage to test a student's ability to comprehend and process spoken information and questions.

If you were a young, lightweight, fearless horseman back in 1860, you might have qualified for a job with the Pony Express. The Pony Express was a mail-delivery service operating between St. Joseph, Missouri and Sacramento, California. The average pay for a rider was $100 per month, but the work was grueling and dangerous. Carrying special saddle-bags for the mail, riders traveled day and night at breakneck speed, through all kinds of weather. Relay stations were set up along the 1900-mile trail, where fresh ponies were ready and waiting. Riders could change horses in about two minutes. An average ride was 75 miles or more, ending at a home station where another rider was waiting.

The Pony Express could deliver mail to California in less than ten days. Their fastest run was in 1861, when President Abraham Lincoln's first address to Congress made it to Sacramento in just seven days.

The opening of the transcontinental telegraph ended the need for the Pony Express. It closed in October, 1861. This was one of the most colorful chapters in the history of the American West.

What put the Pony Express out of business?

A   The invention of the telephone
B   The opening of the transcontinental telegraph
C   The Civil War
D   The San Francisco Earthquake

The correct answer is B.

Which of these is an opinion in this story?

F   The average pay was $100 per month.
G   The Pony Express could deliver mail to California in less than 10 days.
H   This was one of the most colorful chapters in the history of the American West.
J   Riders could change horses in two minutes.

The correct answer is H.

TerraNova

SOME PRODUCTS OF AFRICA—1990s

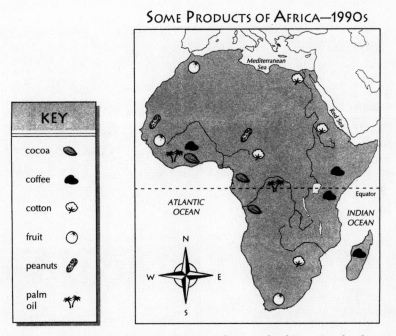

Directions: This map shows some products of Africa. Study the map and key. Then answer Numbers 1 and 2.

According to the map, which of these products is produced farthest east?

A   fruit
B   cocoa
C   coffee
D   peanuts

The correct answer is C.

The map shows some of Africa's

F   capital cities
G   climate patterns
H   mountain ranges
J   agricultural crops

The correct answer is J.

Directions: This picture shows a milk delivery wagon in the late 1800s. Use the picture to do Number 1.

Tell about two clues in the picture that help you know it was taken a long time ago.

READING/ENGLISH/LANGUAGE ARTS

Reading is the central learning skill and therefore a vital component in any set of standardized tests. Reading/language arts exams aim to monitor the student's ability to comprehend process and apply the written word.

The method used to achieve this assessment varies from test to test. These differences parallel the variety of approaches to language acquisition favored by reading experts. You can note this difference in emphasis and style by comparing the Iowa Test of Basic Skills, which tends to the more straightforward and "traditional," with the TerraNova, which is designed to reflect the approach of the newer textbooks currently used across the country.

Following is a selection of sample reading/language arts questions, divided into categories that reflect the concepts or skills being tested.

Reading Comprehension

In the past, the reading comprehension section of standardized tests focused on the student's ability to answer questions about a passage's main idea, purpose, or structure and to draw inferences from the text. Recently, standardized tests also include questions that test a student's vocabulary, spelling, and editing skills, as well as his knowledge of grammar and usage. The theory behind this more comprehensive approach is that since these other language skills are an inherent part of reading comprehension, all these abilities should be tested as a whole.

Here is a representative selection of reading comprehension questions.

TerraNova

Umbrella
by Taro Yashima

On her third birthday
Momo was given two presents—
red rubber boots and an umbrella!
They pleased her so much
that she even woke up that midnight   *midnight = middle*
to take another look at them.   *of the night*
Unfortunately   *unfortunately = sadly*
it was still Indian summer,
and the sun was bright.
Every morning
Momo asked her mother,
who used to take her
to the nearby nursery school,   *nursery school = a school*
"Why the rain doesn't fall?"   *for very young children*
The answer was always the same:
"Wait, wait; it will come."

How does Momo probably feel every morning?

○ tired because   ○ glad because   ○ unhappy because
she wakes up   the sun is bright   she cannot wear
too early   her boots

The correct answer is "unhappy because she cannot wear her boots."

When would it be best for Momo to use her presents?

○   when it's sunny
○   when it's foggy
○   when it's raining

The correct answer is "when it's raining."

What is another word for <u>presents</u>?

○   gifts
○   cards
○   parties

The correct answer is "gifts."

What is <u>not</u> told in the story?

○   who gave the presents to Momo
○   what the presents are
○   how old Momo is

The correct answer is "who gave the presents to Momo."

What does Mother mean when she says, "it will come?"

○   The rain will come.
○   The answer will come.
○   The bus will come.

The correct answer is "The rain will come."

Directions: Read the rhyme. Then do Numbers 1 and 2.

Rain, rain, go away.
Come again another day.

1. Think about Momo from the book <u>Umbrella</u>, by Taro Yashima. Do you think Momo would have said this rhyme? Circle <u>Yes</u> or <u>No</u>

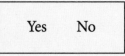

Yes   No

Now write one or two sentences explaining why you think she <u>would</u> or <u>would not</u> like this rhyme.

_____

_____

_____

2. A student wrote two sentences about rain. Each sentence has one mistake. Draw a line through each mistake. Then above the mistake, write that part correctly.

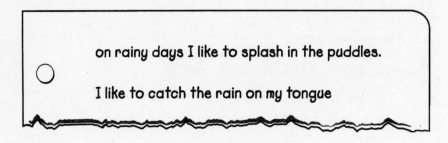

on rainy days I like to splash in the puddles.

I like to catch the rain on my tongue

Iowa Test of Basic Skills

Has a cat ever licked you? If it has, then you know that a cat's tongue doesn't feel smooth and silky. It is covered with hard little bumps.

Cats use their tongues in many ways. They get dirt and loose hair out of their coats with each stroke of their tongues.

Lions, house cats, and other cats also use their tongues to help them loosen meat from bones. Their tongues help them lick the bones clean.

What is this story mostly about?

A   How cats find food
B   Why cats need meat
C   Why cats hunt at night
D   How cats use their tongues

The correct answer is D.

How do cats' tongues feel?

J   Rough
K   Slick
L   Soft
M   Furry

The correct answer is J.

When a cat cleans itself, how does it use its tongue?

J   As a towel
K   As a bathtub
L   As a hairbrush
M   As a bar of soap

The correct answer is L.

TerraNova

Directions: Read the paragraph and look at the web. This web shows how a beaver uses its tail. Use the web to help you answer the questions below.

The Beaver

The beaver uses its tail in many ways. It slaps the water with its tail to signal danger. It also steers with its tail as it swims. The beaver props itself up with its tail when it stands up to gnaw on tree trunks. Finally, the beaver uses its tail to pat mud into place around the logs of its lodge.

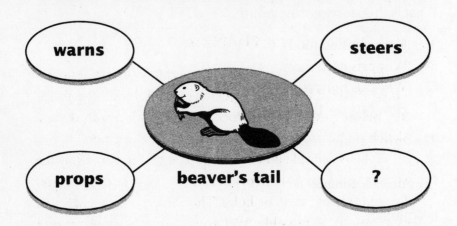

Which of these words should be added to the empty circle to show one more use of the beaver's tail?

A   pats
B   grinds
C   climbs
D   chops

The correct answer is A.

Which phrase or idea from the passage supports your answer choice in the previous question?

F   steers with its tail
G   uses its tail to pat mud
H   props itself up with its tail
J   slaps the water with its tail

The correct answer is G.

Directions: People in Mexico and Guatemala have been making pottery for thousands of years. Here is a passage from a book about Mexican customs that tells about making pottery. Read the passage. Then do Numbers 1 through 6.

Clay Pottery

You can find Mexican pottery clay in most arts and crafts stores. This red, moist clay hardens by drying in the air. Before you begin to work, it is a good idea to draw a sketch of the pot you want to make to use as a guide.

To make simple pinch pots, start with a lump of clay the size of a tennis ball. Working on a flat, smooth surface, knead it to get rid of air holes. Then shape it into a ball that is as round as possible. Wet your thumb with water and press it into the top of the clay ball. Turn the pot with your other hand. Press the sides up and out. Sides should be about 1/4 inch (6 mm) thick. Keep the walls uniform and do not make the base too thick or the rim too thin. Smooth the pot on the inside and outside. When it is finished, let the pot dry at room temperature away from heat. When it is dry, you can decorate it with paint or leave it plain. To make coil pots, form ropes of clay and stack and shape them. Knead them together. You can leave them as they are, with ridges showing, or smooth them with wet fingers.

---

1. This passage is mostly about

A   how pottery is used in art
B   how to make clay pots
C   artists who make pottery
D   different ways to decorate pots

The correct answer is B.

Here are two sentences related to the passage:

> *She made a vase out of clay.*
> *The clay was red.*

2. Which of these best combines the two sentences into one?

F   She made a vase out of red clay.
G   She made a vase out of clay, and the clay was red.
H   She made a red vase out of clay.
J   She made a vase out of clay, the clay was red.

The correct answer is F.

3. According to the passage, if you were making a pinch pot, what could you do after you smooth the pot and leave it to dry?

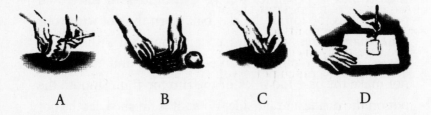

A   B   C   D

The correct answer is A, the illustration of someone painting a completed pinch pot.

4. Which of these describes the best way to find the answer to Number 3?

F   scanning the passage for the section that describes smoothing the pot
G   looking for the title of the passage
H   re-reading the passage to find the main idea
J   outlining the passage and detailing each step

The correct answer is F.

> The wet clay pot _____.

5. Choose the word that means that the pot caved in.

A   shattered
B   collapsed
C   evaporated
D   dissolved

The correct answer is B.

6. Which sentence is complete and written correctly?

F   Molding a pinch pot out of clay.
G   Work on a good surface, the pot can be made more easily.
H   The moist clay drying in the air.
J   After making a pinch pot, try making a coil pot, too.

The correct answer is J.

Directions: Use the passage and the diagram below to answer the question.

In both men's and women's basketball competition, a basic defense is the *zone* defense. In this strategy, a defensive player stays in his/her own zone or area and tries to maintain a position between the basket and any offensive player who enters that zone. An offensive player can move all over the court.

Look at the diagram. If the players in black uniforms are constantly moving from one zone to another, they are probably

A   offensive players who are leaving the game
B   defensive players trying to block their opponents' shots
C   offensive players who are maneuvering for a shot at the basket
D   defensive players trying to confuse the offensive team

The correct answer is C.

Directions: We will listen in as some students interview Dr. Theodore A. Reyman, a pathologist who specializes in examining mummies for scientific purposes.

Dr. Theodore A. Reyman

Q *Dr. Reyman, what exactly is a mummy?*

A A mummy is simply a preserved body that still has some soft tissue remaining. It is different from a skeleton, which is all bones. Mummies do not have to be ancient, but most of the ones we study are over two thousand years old. We know that some societies practiced mummification of their dead for thousands of years.

Q *Are there different kinds of mummies?*

A Yes, bodies can be naturally mummified by dry desert heat or by freezing, but most mummies we study had been intentionally prepared for burial by using elaborate preservation methods.

Q *You are a medical doctor. Why do you study mummies?*

A I study mummies because they have something to say about the history of human disease. If we understand how diseases change over long periods of time, we might learn how diseases develop and spread. With this knowledge, we are better equipped to treat, cure, and perhaps even wipe out some diseases.

Q *Dr. Reyman, where do the mummies for your research come from?*

A Well, we have worked on mummies from Egypt, China, Peru, the American Southwest, Alaska, and Siberia. The Egyptian mummies we studied were loaned to us by museums.

Q *It must be spooky and scary to work on ancient bodies! Don't they smell terrible when you unwrap them?*

A Despite what you might think, there were never any scary moments. And the mummies we worked on never had any offensive odors. In fact, they sometimes had the fragrance of cedar resin (sap) or of old spices.

Q *How do you treat a mummy when it is being examined?*

A To begin with, each mummy must be approached as if it were the last one on earth, and each one is treated with the utmost respect. Only the most meager samples of skin and muscle are gingerly snipped off for analysis because the mummies are later returned to museums for display.

Q *You must have been given a lot of praise and encouragement for starting such important research.*

A No, in fact some doctors and scientists thought this type of study was a complete waste of time, that we could not possibly find any useful information. The encouragement I did receive was from my father when I was growing up. He taught me to be eager to learn and to seek out the truth, that there is a reason for everything.

Q *Were there any major disappointments or setbacks in your research on mummies?*

A Yes, there were. Basically, we were looking for microscopic antibodies that would show which infectious diseases a person had been exposed to. We did not have any success on the first two mummies, so we were almost to the point of thinking it was useless. Then, on our third try, using the mummy we called PUM-2, we found the serum protein we were looking for. Our knowledge of ancient diseases and how they relate to modern diseases has grown steadily since then.

Q *Dr. Reyman, how do you feel about your career choices now?*

A I realize how lucky I have been to be able to participate in this work. But there is so much more to learn. Given the chance, I would do it all over again, but I'd start sooner!

What was Dr. Reyman's main motivation for becoming involved with research on mummies?

A   He hoped to receive recognition for his work.
B   He hoped to obtain knowledge about human disease.
C   He wanted to increase interest in mummies and their history.
D   He wanted to find new ways to preserve bodies.

The correct answer is B.

Why do you think some doctors and scientists said Dr. Reyman's research would be a waste of time?

F   They thought it had been done before.
G   They felt jealous when not asked to participate.
H   They didn't like to work on mummies.
J   They couldn't foresee the value of his work.

The correct answer is J.

Dr. Reyman says that the mummies sometimes had the *fragrance* of spices. Which of the following words means about the same as *fragrance?*

A   texture
B   aroma
C   taste
D   stench

The correct answer is B.

Meager samples of skin and muscle were snipped for laboratory samples. Which of the following words means about the same as *meager?*

F   diseased
G   abundant
H   minuscule
J   cautious

The correct answer is H.

Which evidence from the interview best supports the definition you chose for the previous question?

A   Mummies often must be put back on display in museums after scientists examine them.
B   Mummies can be produced by dry desert heat.
C   Mummies have been found all over the world.
D   Mummies sometimes have the fragrance of cedar resin.

The correct answer is A.

After listening to Dr. Reyman discuss the examination of two mummies, a student wrote this report. Read the first half of the report.

> 1) Dr. Reyman once examined a well-preserved teenage boy named Nakht. 2) He had been a weaver in the royal temple at Thebes in Egypt about 3200 years ago. 3) He must have been a good weaver to be in the royal temple. 4) Dr. Reyman was able to identify the disease that killed him. 5) This disease was caused by a parasite that is still a widespread medical problem in Egypt today.

Which sentence does not belong in the paragraph?

F   Sentence 2
G   Sentence 3
H   Sentence 4
J   Sentence 5

The correct answer is G.

Spelling

Iowa Test of Basic Skills

Which of the following words is misspelled?

J eightey
K besides
L thanked
M warmer
N *(No mistakes)*

The correct answer is J.

Stanford Achievement Test, Intermediate

Which of the following underlined words is incorrect?

A A <u>flower</u> grew in the garden.
B This song <u>seams</u> very long.
C Adam has <u>thrown</u> the rock.
D No mistake

The correct answer is B.

F The <u>palace</u> is on a high hill.
G What <u>type</u> of car is it?
H We <u>beleive</u> in you.
J No mistake

The correct answer is H.

Vocabulary/Word Usage

Iowa Test of Basic Skills

For each question, you are to decide which one of the four answers has most nearly the same meaning as the underlined word above it.

A <u>mighty</u> wind

A   cold
B   steady
C   strong
D   nighttime

The correct answer is C.

Phonetics/Reading

Stanford Achievement Test, Primary 2

The following questions are read aloud by the teacher, and are designed to test student's ability to understand spoken language and translate it into the written word.

> Find the word that is made up of two words.

tomorrow   shoelace   different
  ○   ○   ○

The correct answer is choice 2.

Mark under *paints*. The girl *paints* a picture.

painting   painter   paints
  ○   ○   ○

The correct answer is choice 3.

Capitalization

Iowa Test of Basic Skills

You should look for mistakes in capitalization in this sentence.

J   Daniel couldn't go to school
K   on Friday, so his sister got his
L   Homework from Mr. Johnson.
M   *(No mistakes)*

The correct answer is L.

Grammar/Usage

Iowa Test of Basic Skills

You should look for mistakes in the way words are used in these sentences.

A   Bill collects the same baseball
B   cards I do. Him has the biggest
C   collection in the third grade.
D   (No mistakes)

The correct answer is B.

A   Doug spent the night with us
B   while his parents were gone. He
C   had the mostest fun of his life.
D   (No mistakes)

The correct answer is C.

Stanford Achievement Test, Primary 2

> "Akim hurt his foot. On a nail." How should this group of words be written? Should it be *Akim hurt his foot on a nail.* . . . *Akim hurting his foot on a nail.* . . . or is the group of words okay *The way it is?*

Akim hurt his foot. On a nail.

- ○   Akim hurt his foot on a nail.
- ○   Akim hurting his foot on a nail.
- ○   The way it is

The correct answer is choice 1.

> "I spilled my juice and then cleaned it up." How should this group of words be written? Should it be *Spilling my juice and then cleaning it up.... I spilled my juice. And then cleaned it up....* or should it be written *The way it is?*

I spilled my juice and then cleaned it up.

- ○   Spilling my juice and then cleaning it up.
- ○   I spilled my juice. And then cleaned it up.
- ○   The way it is

The correct answer is choice 3.

Reasoning

Stanford Achievement Test, Intermediate

Smiling Jack promised the job of ship's cook to the first person to arrive at the ship on Saturday morning.

Using the statement of the cooks, find out what time each arrived at the ship. On the lines under their pictures below, write the time that each cook arrived. Then number the cooks from 1 to 7 to show the order in which they arrived.

Carol Catnip	David Dill	Gary Garlic	Molly Mint	Peter Pumpkin	Sally Saffron	Wally Watercress
_____	_____	_____	_____	_____	_____	_____

Communication

Stanford Achievement Test, Intermediate

These cartoons show what happened when Smiling Jack stopped at Treasure Cove to buy supplies. Jack is talking to a shop clerk. In each cartoon, fill in the speech "balloons" so that the cartoon makes mathematical sense.

At the Sailor Shop

At the Boatyard

Writing Assessment

These open-ended writing assessment questions from the Stanford Achievement Test, Primary 3 are examples of how standardized tests assess writing ability. They present simple scenarios, and ask the student to produce responses in four "modes" of writing: descriptive, narrative, expository, and persuasive.

Descriptive

Think about a toy that you like. It might be a toy that you have played with or one that you have seen. Tell what the toy is, and **describe** what it looks like so that someone who has not seen it could picture it.

Narrative

Think about a time when you helped someone or someone helped you. Write a story about what happened.

Expository

If you had ten dollars to spend in any way you wanted, what would you buy? Be sure to tell **why** you would spend the money that way and **explain** your reasons.

Persuasive

Imagine that your teacher has announced that your class has enough money to take a one-day field trip. Where should the class go on the field trip? Write a letter to **convince** your teacher to pick the place you have chosen. Be sure to tell **why** you chose that place and **explain** your reasons.

You should begin and end your letter like this:

Dear Teacher:

Sincerely,

A Student

DURING THE TEST: TIPS AND GUIDELINES

Now that you've reviewed the sample questions, and you're pre-pared and ready to go, here are a few final suggestions to convey to your child that will help her during the test. You might want to mention them casually several days before the exam and remind her of some of these pointers again on the morning of the test.

Answer All the Questions

Most standardized tests do not take off points for wrong answers. (A few do—the SAT College Entrance Exam, for instance; but most, if not all, elementary and middle school standardized tests do not penalize for incorrect choices.) We hope that your child's teacher has already made this clear, but it's worth repeating. After all, why lose needless points? Make sure your child knows to leave a few extra minutes during which he can fill in all the blanks on the question sheet.

How should he guess? A common question about random guessing is whether it is a better strategy to jump around and select letters "a" to "e" or to stick with one letter—say, "c"—all the way down. The answer is: it doesn't matter. Presumably, the test selections on these tests are randomly apportioned, and, therefore, one's guesses ought to be random as well. Statistically, one tactic is as good as the other.

Listen to Instructions

Again and again, we hear stories about smart kids who do poorly on standardized tests because they misunderstood what was required of them. You're a parent so we don't have to tell you that kids and instructions rarely mix well together. Take pains, therefore, to remind your child to pay close attention to the teacher's instruc-tions. This includes disabusing him of the usual assumption that he knows what to do on these tests—didn't he just take one a few months ago? Explain that standardized tests come in various formats. Make sure, too, that your child is prepared for the teacher's mechanized reading of the instructions and understands that the officious tone is part of the test rules.

That's the listening part. He will also read the instructions when the test booklet is distributed. And he should read all of it—especially the sample question and answer, if they are provided. He should feel free to ask the teacher for guidance if the instructions are not clear. This isn't the time to suddenly become shy.

Practice Time Management

It isn't obvious to children that they should abandon a question just because they are having a difficult time arriving at the answer. Many will just plug away until they are satisfied. This is an admirable trait in ordinary circumstances, but not on a timed exam. You want your child to feel as if she has adequate time to answer all the questions, but not to be oblivious to the ticking of the clock. Tell your child that if a question is too complicated, she ought to let it be and move on to the next, hopefully easier, question. At the end of the test, if time remains, she can go back and have another try at the question that gave her trouble.

Read All the Choices

This, too, is a piece of advice especially appropriate for children. Test-taking savvy comes with experience, and young students haven't yet acquired the reasonable suspicion that comes with years of taking exams: test-makers do try to trick you. They systematically throw in choices that are nearly, but not quite, the right answer; plausible, reasonable choices—but wrong. When one of these deceptive, false answers is among the first couple of choices, a student can easily get snared and choose it without proceeding to the later, correct alternative.

So emphasize the importance of examining all the possible answers, even when you've found the right one.

Never and Always

This isn't an absolute rule and should not be followed absolutely, but—answers that contain absolutes are often incorrect. Sentences that contain such words as "never" or "always" are more often false (let's stress again: often, not definitely). Exceptions are the rule in life. The absolute advice here, therefore, is to be especially careful when choosing an answer that allows for no exceptions.

Yes, Change Your Answer

There's a myth floating around that your first selection on a test is always the right one. Not necessarily. Your child should feel free to change her answer if it seems on reflection that she should. One reason why this myth is so popular is that we tend to remember with chagrin those times we changed our answers from the right one to the wrong one, but forget the many times we went from a wrong answer to the correct one.

The point is that no hard-and-fast rules apply here. If your original answer now seems less convincing, by all means switch to another. The only thing your child should not second-guess is herself, once she's handed in her paper.

Review Your Answer Sheet

This is a clean-up chore. Remind your child to check that each answer bubble has been filled in with a dark pencil marking and that no question has two answers—that's automatic points off. Remind him, as well, to look for and erase stray pencil marks; the computer may interpret these markings as incorrect responses.

Leave When You're Finished

Not before. But you needn't wait around either. Some children think it's admirable to be among the first to complete the exam.

Other students get nervous when they are done but see their classmates still toiling away—"Have I missed something?" they wonder.

Your child should understand that taking standardized tests is not a group activity. He shouldn't rush: use all the time he needs. But when he's convinced he's done and checked his answers, he should feel free to hand in his work.

One more piece of advice: Your child should also be aware that many tests are designed *not* to be completed.

When It's Over, It's Over

Don't harp on the test. When your child comes home, ask her how it went. If she wants to talk about it in detail, listen. If she mutters "fine" and quickly retreats to her play station, let her be. Your child's comfort level about the test should dictate your own response.

Chapter 5

♦

The Envelope Please: When the Test Results Are In

Marcia has trouble steadying her coffee cup. "Relax, this is silly," she says, trying to calm herself. "I'm sure Danielle did very well, and if she didn't, there's always next time." Marcia isn't very convincing. Several minutes pass before she takes a deep breath and reaches for the letter sitting on the table beside her.

Marcia believes that the test scores in her hand present a fairly accurate indication of her 11-year-old daughter's academic abilities. She also believes that no matter what they say officially, the exam results influence the school administrators' and teachers' estimation of Danielle. For Marcia, standardized tests matter a great deal.

Eric's response to the test is the polar opposite of Marcia's. He takes a quick look at the results and doesn't even bother to read the footnotes that explain how to interpret the numbers. "Why should I? These scores don't mean diddley-squat," he says. "No two-hour short-answer test can tell you how smart or stupid a kid is. I know my son Mike is a bright kid and so do his teachers. I'm sure the only reason the school even bothers going through the motions is because of some bureaucratic requirement."

Neither Marcia's overwhelming anxiety nor Eric's underwhelming disregard is a reasonable reaction. As with most of life's hurdles, the sensible course is moderation, an approach in-between the extremes of these two parents. Your reaction to your child's performance is not, however, the only reaction that matters. How the school and your child deal with the test results is also of importance. And you, dear parent, have a significant role to play in their response as well as your own.

TAKE THESE RESULTS SERIOUSLY

Let's begin with you, the parent, and with some unadorned, unobscured, unsentimental truths.

You know your child very well, better than anyone else. That's the problem. We know only our own children very well, and maybe a few other children somewhat, but that's hardly an ample sample from which to draw conclusions about what children of a particular age should be expected to know.

Let's be clear: all the abilities and achievements measured by these tests are at root comparisons. A question like, "Does Sam read well?" either invites the question "Compared with whom?" or the question "Compared with what standard?" In judging your child's reading ability, say, we are comparing his abilities to the norm of other eighth graders in the country or to the appropriate reading level of an eighth grader as determined by reading specialists. In either case, we need a large representative sample to establish this yardstick.

So to some extent Marcia does have it right. When a million eighth grade students from across the country take a test, we get a good idea of the average skill of eighth graders. A parent might believe that her child has an outstanding gift for mathematics or, alternatively, a deficient one, but if the child's scores are consistently smack in the middle of the national average, the parent should reassess her assumption.

Let's also be honest about something else. When you evaluate your children, you can't help but judge them through the filter of your personal biases. We pay attention to the facilities of children that we think are important and ignore skills that we don't especially value. For example, a parent might believe that knowing how to compose a solid, grammatical sentence is critical to one's education, but that developing a large vocabulary is only a minor aspiration. A well-designed standardized test,

> *We throw all our attention on the utterly idle question of whether A has done as well as B when the only question is whether A has done as well as he could.*
> *—William Graham Sumner*

however, probes an array of capacities deemed essential by learning experts and tests for these proficiencies with equal impartiality. The cold objectivity of the standardized test is one of its chief merits.

And unlike other class exams or the impromptu quizzes you hurl at your child during dinner, standardized tests do not have a direct instructional purpose. Their principal function is to measure the test-taker's achievement or aptitude against a norm or an established standard. What you, the parent, or the school does with these results is not the business of the test publisher. It is your business.

To those who belittle test scores, Marcia's allies hurl a final psychological parry. "'Kill the messenger' is an entrenched human response to bearers of bad news," they remind us. No doubt, you can recall making light of a poor test showing by dismissing the exam as unfair or by claiming that the test happened to focus on precisely those areas you didn't study. We're apt to respond the same way when our child scores low—we de-legitimate the test. Of course, when our child scores high, we are quick to declare that the test accurately reflects our progeny's gigantic intellectual prowess.

Standardized test scores are certainly not meaningless. They convey information that can be very useful in fine-tuning your child's education. On the other hand, this sober appreciation of these tests should be tempered with some of Eric's doubts.

BUT NOT TOO SERIOUSLY

Yes, it's true. Some brilliant kids don't do brilliantly on standardized tests. (Although, let's quickly add, they rarely do terribly.) An average score by no means proves average ability. Some children choke at exams. Anyone can have a bad day. It would be unfair for a teacher to give a young student a final grade based on a single test. But standardized tests do not allow for a second chance.

Critics of standardized tests also express dissatisfaction with the level of diagnosis provided by the short-answer format. Pick up any popular magazine, they say, and you can see how superficial multiple-choice questions can be. For example, a typical quiz to help you determine your "romance quotient" asks which of the following scenarios most entices you: a) a week in a hut with letter-bomb killer Theodore Kaczynski, b) a body massage by Linda Tripp, c) an in-depth discussion about monetary policy and the budget deficit with Dennis Rodman, or d) three plush evenings in Paris with the lover of your choice. Duh.

The usual multiple-choice format of even the best standardized assessment, say the tests' detractors, can't dig deep enough to examine how a student thinks about a problem or decipher the process by which he arrives at an answer. The capacity to learn is a complex notion: one student's average score might mean something entirely different from another student's average score. This reminds one of the statistician who had one foot in the oven and the other foot in the freezer and announced, "On average I feel fine." We need to know the ingredients that form the child's results.

Defenders of Eric's skepticism also point out that standardized test scores are tainted because some schools "teach to the test." Schools are under increasing pressure to have their students score

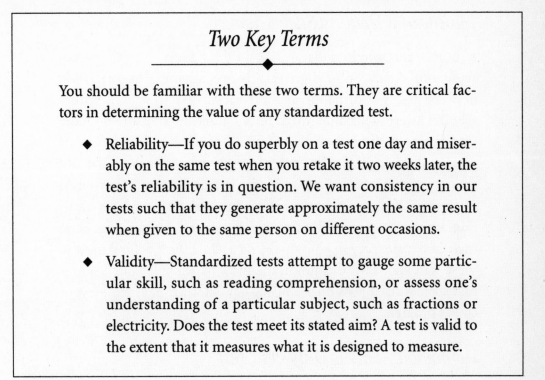

Two Key Terms

You should be familiar with these two terms. They are critical factors in determining the value of any standardized test.

- ◆ Reliability—If you do superbly on a test one day and miserably on the same test when you retake it two weeks later, the test's reliability is in question. We want consistency in our tests such that they generate approximately the same result when given to the same person on different occasions.

- ◆ Validity—Standardized tests attempt to gauge some particular skill, such as reading comprehension, or assess one's understanding of a particular subject, such as fractions or electricity. Does the test meet its stated aim? A test is valid to the extent that it measures what it is designed to measure.

well and, accordingly, develop curricula geared to the test and encourage teachers to expend time and energy reviewing test-taking skills. At the same time, some schools don't bother at all with preparing their students for these tests. As a result, these norms and standards, they argue, are not genuine.

SOME SENSIBLE CONCLUSIONS

Based on recent studies on the impact of standardized test results, the following considerations should inform your own attitude toward these tests.

The Scores Do Deserve Your Careful Attention

Don't ignore them because of cynicism, arrogance, or insecurity. You do your child no favor by disregarding his performance on these tests.

Maintain a Healthy Skepticism

Educational researchers disagree about the value of even the best of standardized tests. Some claim that there is a significant correlation between test performance and future success in school. Other scholars assert that standardized tests still mostly measure no more than how well one does on these tests.

As educational professionals ourselves, we want to flat-out assure you that when you read a report claiming that a "consensus of experts" believes that standardized tests are "undeniably accurate" or, conversely, that they are "clearly useless" … well, there is no such consensus. As you know, political agendas lurk behind most of these statements. At this point, the most reasonable conclusion is that standardized tests can be of substantial value in assessing your child's progress.

Remember, This Is Only One Test

No one examination can give you a comprehensive and definitive profile of your child's intellectual status—these are at best snapshots of a student's abilities. Put this test result into the hopper along with all the other indicators of your child's output—his class work, his teacher's feedback, his interest in learning, and a host of other subjective criteria. Be on notice for sharp discrepancies. And don't be surprised if you find them for, as the wise Chinese aphorism observes, "He with one watch knows the time, but he with two isn't sure."

Maintain Focus

Your child wasn't given this test so that you can gloat or, alternatively, despair. Sure, it's only natural that you'll feel proud if she excelled and worried if she did poorly, but get over it. The purpose of providing you with the test results is to help you help your child enrich her areas of strength and improve her areas of weakness. The test may not be designed as an instructional tool, but you can turn it into one.

UNDERSTANDING THE TEST RESULTS

In this section, we'll walk you through the process of interpreting the results of a typical standardized test. Relax. We promise that we do not assume that you have an advanced degree in statistics; undoubtedly, students will have a more difficult challenge taking their test than you'll have reading the results.

These days, interpreting test results is becoming a lot easier thanks to the snazzy charts and helpful tips that accompany the scores—this is one way publishing companies enhance the marketing appeal of their test products.

The graphics help, but they don't take you off the hook completely: you still need to understand what these results actually measure. To help you decipher standardized scores, let's look at the hypothetical test result belonging to 10-year-old Oscar on page 118.

What Do All These Numbers Mean?

The first figure we need to explain is the one that follows Oscar's grade. It reads 4.6, which means fourth year, sixth month of the school year; Oscar took this test in the sixth month (probably February) of his stint in the fourth grade.

Now let's look at his raw scores. These refer to the actual number of questions that Oscar answered correctly in this part of the

---

A Reminder about Keeping Your Focus

◆

This is just a gentle, quick reminder about the point of this whole operation. You're not directly concerned at the moment with the state of education in the United States, nor even with how well your child's school district compares with others. Your immediate interest is your child and noting his or her strengths and weaknesses. That's primarily what you'll be looking for in reviewing these test results.

Sample Test Score

◆

NAME: OSCAR FELIXSON
GRADE: 4.6
DATE OF BIRTH: 12/16/88

SKILLS

READING COMPREHENSION

Raw Score	Percentile Ranking	Grade Equivalence	Stanine
35	50	4.0	5

VOCABULARY

Raw Score	Percentile Ranking	Grade Equivalence	Stanine
37	54	4.3	6

MATH CONCEPTS

Raw Score	Percentile Ranking	Grade Equivalence	Stanine
32	54	3.9	5

MATH COMPUTATION

Raw Score	Percentile Ranking	Grade Equivalence	Stanine
27	46	3.7	4

test. But this number in isolation tells you nothing. Oscar got 35 right answers in his reading comprehension. But 35 out of what? If out of 40, his results are pretty good, but if they're 35 out of a possible 200, they're a disaster. You should pay attention to the raw score only if you are also given the total number of questions asked in each section.

Let's look at the next column, the national percentile ranking. A percentile provides a statistical ranking of your child's performance compared with hundreds of thousands of other children in his or her norm group. Percentiles, as usual, are based on a 100% scale, so if Oscar's ranking is 46% in math computation, that means that 54% of the norm group scored higher than he did—or, to put a happier face on this, 46% scored lower. This score might not mean much if all other indications suggest that Oscar is doing fine in math computation, but absent this evidence, Oscar's parents should certainly pay close attention to the development of his math skills.

What's a Norm Group?

You may have noticed how we slipped in the term "norm group" in the preceding paragraph. We're not going to test you on reading comprehension (lucky you) but just in case you're faking it and aren't really sure what a norm group is, let's review that concept. It's a critical feature of standardized tests.

A norm group is a set of students chosen to represent a designated population. This group could be students in the Northeast, say, or students in urban schools or private schools. In principle, a norm group could be demarcated as children with blue-streaked hair who have pierced belly-buttons and an abiding love of Haydn sonatas. In the real world, test publishers are interested in creating a representative norm group that can serve as a useful basis of comparison for most children and, therefore, are careful to use norm groups that are racially and geographically diverse.

For example, part of the success of the TerraNova, a standardized test used throughout California and other states, is due to the test publisher's inclusion in its "norm" of students from both public and Catholic schools, students from stratified geographic areas and communities (urban, suburban, and rural), and students from representative district sizes (various average enrollments).

One important advantage of a well-established norm group is that you don't have to compare your child's scores with other parents in the class. The percentile ranking tells you how well he or she did compared with a much larger sample of like students.

Your Legal Right as a Parent

◆

Perhaps you've lost your child's test scores from years past and would like to see a record of these results. Or maybe something tells you that the school has different scores for your child than the ones you have. Whatever the reason, you have a right to your child's school records. This includes everything from teacher reports, class grades, and discipline notices to standardized test scores.

The Family Educational Rights and Privacy Act—also known as FERPA or the The Buckley Amendment—regulates this parental right of access. Teachers have this right too, as do school officials, and schools to which a student applies or wishes to transfer, but these personnel and institutions must obtain written parental permission to get this information. Parents, moreover, not only have the right to view their child's reports, they also have the right to correct inaccurate information in those reports.

These records are obviously important to a child's progress in school. Information is added to students' folders as they proceed from grade to grade, school to school, and even as they move on to

---

Okay . . . on then to the next set of figures.

Grade equivalence. As with Oscar's grade at the time of the test, these numbers are usually joined by a colon or period. The first number represents the grade level, the second the month of the school year. In vocabulary, Oscar scored a 4.3, that is, fourth grade, third month. Since he took the test in the sixth month of the fourth grade, on this measure he's about three months below average—not great, but not terrible. If Oscar has responsible parents, they'll drag him away from the play station and bring him more often to the library.

The fourth column is the stanine score. Stanine scores are a nine-point scale that measures performance against a designated

---

Your Legal Right as a Parent (continued)

◆

college. Inaccuracies could have a serious effect: teachers might, as a result, overestimate or underestimate a student's potential. A child could be placed in the wrong class or, more generally, placed on the wrong "academic track," and colleges might, as a consequence, unfairly reject a student's application.

So if you think it is warranted, do check your child's records. The procedure is fairly simple. Call the school office. Be specific about what you want to see. (By the way, some schools charge a small processing fee for this.) Block out time to peruse the report— usually, a half-hour should be enough. Note: you are not permitted to remove the records from the school, but you can make copies. If you do find a significant mistake, make a written request of the school to have the information corrected and follow up to make sure that it has.

Schools must comply within 45 days to your request or lose their right to government funding. If you run into problems, call your state Department of Education.

---

norm group. Thus, 1, 2, and 3 are below average; 4, 5, and 6 are average; and 7, 8, and 9 are above average. Sometimes the stanine norm group will be a national representative group, but often stanines are matched against a smaller subset. For example, many independent private schools have their own stanine standards—that is, a student's score might place her in the upper regions of the percentile range when measured against all students, but only average when compared with other students in independent private schools.

Oscar's stanine score is matched against the general norm, so his number is another way of looking at his percentile score. He received a stanine "4" in mathematical computation, which indicates that he's low-average in this ability.

Oscar's Big Picture

So . . . how's Oscar doing? As we've said repeatedly, no one test can answer that. But one good standardized test can give you some important clues.

> *You cannot teach a man anything. You can only help him discover it himself.*
> —*Galileo*

Based on these scores, Oscar seems to be doing fair in reading comprehension and vocabulary, but somewhat less well in math. In truth, he's scored below grade expectations in each of the four areas tested, but not dramatically so. For a concerned parent, this is certainly useful information. The remaining chapters will suggest how to use this information to improve your child's test-taking ability—and overall education.

Chapter 6

◆

Will the Test Scores Really Matter?

All this fretting about the test and finally the results are in. What happens now? How will these scores be used by your child's school?

In some cases, the results don't count for much at all—they follow precisely the pattern of your child's performance in school and on previous tests. But sometimes the results can matter a great deal—your child's scores may be the decisive factor in determining whether he gets promoted or is tracked into an accelerated learning program. You can influence these decisions, but only if you understand the system—who makes what judgments and on what basis.

KEY ELEMENTS OF THE PROCESS

Let's look at some of the key elements of the decision process:

◆ The type of test administered
◆ The range of subjects tested
◆ The score format requested by the school

- ◆ The teacher's training in interpreting standardized test results
- ◆ How closely the test tracks the curriculum
- ◆ The time elapsed between taking the test and getting the results
- ◆ State, district, and individual school policies
- ◆ National education goals and standards

Type of Test

By now—and certainly by the time you finish reading this book—you'll be familiar with the two main types of standardized tests: norm-referenced and criterion-referenced. Norm-referenced tests, remember, tell you how well your child did on a given test compared with other children of the same age and grade. Criterion-referenced tests measure how well your child has mastered a level of knowledge considered standard for his grade. Aptitude tests that measure cognitive skills and potential ability are norm-referenced. Achievement tests that measure subject knowledge can fall into either category.

In response to the national pressure to raise school standards, the trend of late has been toward increased use of criterion-referenced standardized tests. Many states and school districts, however, are taking a combined approach: administering criterion-referenced achievement tests and norm-referenced aptitude tests developed in tandem. Popular examples of this joint assessment are the Stanford Achievement Test and the Otis-Lennon School Ability Test and The Iowa Test of Basic Skills and Cognitive Abilities Test. (See Chapter 3 for a full discussion of these—and other—tests.)

Test scores on linked achievement/aptitude tests can be especially informative and enable teachers and parents to more easily identify discrepancies in a child's progress. But because many schools do not offer linked tests, the divergence may go unnoticed by the school. The responsibility for keeping track of different results, therefore, is yours.

Range of Subjects Tested

What subjects will be covered in your child's standardized exams this year? He may be given the full battery: criterion-referenced and norm-referenced tests together with other open-ended assessments, on subjects that cover the pedagogical waterfront, from language skills, reading comprehension, and writing to science, mathematics, and social studies. The more likely scenario, however, is that your child will take standardized tests in only a few selected areas. The main reasons for this limited assessment are time and money: test publishers charge considerable fees for administering and scoring exams, and time devoted to test-taking is time taken away from classroom education.

The range of subjects tested, therefore, will determine, in part, the impact of standardized test scores on your child. The more areas tested, the better picture the school has of your child's learning profile, and the more inclined they are to base their decisions about your child's educational needs on these exams.

Types of Score Reports

Scoring is also a business. The schools not only select which tests to administer from among the many on the market, but also choose the form in which the results are reported. Available formats range from the boilerplate to the graphically sophisticated and detailed. As you might expect, the more complex the report, the more expensive.

Here's the problem for parents. Test reports are designed for targeted audiences—typically the district supervisors and school administrators who pay for these reports. Since the primary purpose of statewide testing programs is to track and compare general school performance and aggregate student achievement, the score reports tend to address these specific interests.

Although these reports may lack the specific individual information that parents would like to see, they do provide important data about each child's performance. Your job is to understand how to read these results (as we explained in Chapter 5) so that your discussions with the school staff are informative and effective.

Has Your Child's Teacher Been Trained to Interpret Test Scores?

Fact: Some teachers are trained to analyze test scores and do so intelligently; others lack this training and make inferences about your child's ability that are no more than guesses. Mind you, this lack of training isn't the teacher's fault—instruction costs time and money, and most schools are strapped for both.

It's important that you recognize this range of expertise. Try to find out whether the person scoring the test has been trained to do so—but please be subtle! And note, too, that since many of these tests are new, even teachers with years of experience scoring standardized tests may find themselves swimming in uncharted waters. Take their conclusions seriously, but not as the final law. (Indeed, after reading this book, your own interpretation of your child's test results may be as much on target as theirs.)

If your child's teacher is, in fact, trained in reading standardized tests, then take her opinions all the more seriously. Don't shy away from offering your own appraisal, but be willing to defer to the teacher if she demonstrates a better understanding of the scores.

In any case, make sure your discussion proceeds not from an adversarial stance but from a recognition of your mutually supportive, shared goals. Working together, you and the teacher can be forceful advocates for the best educational interests of your child.

Is the Test Related to the Curriculum?

Norm-referenced standardized tests reflect the curriculum only to a limited degree. Cognitive tests, such as IQ tests, which are designed to measure innate ability rather than content, are even further removed from the curriculum taught to your child. (Of course, a more challenging program of study improves thinking; but the test score in itself won't shed much light on the depth of the curriculum.)

Criterion-referenced standardized tests, on the other hand, are more directly tied to curriculum; they measure, for example, how well a student has mastered essential reading and math skills. The current push for national standardized tests is part of a campaign to raise national educational standards, and, therefore, more and more states are administering these criterion-referenced tests. By the time your child gets to high school, a content-based standardized test may be required for graduation; a few states have already adopted this policy, and many others are considering doing the same.

Can you do anything about your child's school curriculum? That depends on who chooses the curriculum. When it is the state or the school district, even the teachers must follow the stipulated curriculum and have very little room for their own preferences—you as a parent have even less influence in shaping the course of study. In these circumstances, if your child scored poorly on the standardized test, your best option may be remedial help. If you can't change the curriculum, change your child's study habits. When the teacher does have latitude on what gets taught, low scores across the class should prompt a reconsideration, though not necessarily the elimination, of the current instructional program.

When Do the Scores Arrive?

Unfortunately, the time between the day a standardized test is taken and the results are received can be considerable. Even in this computerized age, the scoring process is time-consuming. Here's a rule of thumb: the less standardized the test, the longer you'll have to wait for the results. Not surprisingly, multiple-choice tests that simply require filling in answers on a machine-scoreable sheet are returned more quickly than open-ended performance assessment tests that ask for written explanations and writing samples. These open-ended assessments may be graded by your child's teacher or another specialist in the school trained in test scoring. The drawback here, once again, is the length of time it takes to arrive at the results.

Grading open-ended tests is a laborious process. In New York City, for example, open-ended performance assessments are given in science and math, usually in February or March, and are then kept under lock and key in the principal's office. As one fifth grade teacher reports, because the tests can be scored only on school premises and only during specially designated times, she has just two afternoons in the four months following the test day to grade more than 30 tests. The results, therefore, aren't available until the very end of the school year.

Although this teacher likes open-ended tests because "they have the advantage of allowing students to construct their own answers to questions, as in the real world, and therefore provide greater insight into the critical thinking and problem-solving skills of the respective students," she finds the time lag in scoring these tests disconcerting. "Unless I steal the tests from the principal's office and score them at home, I won't get the results until it's too late to be of much use to me in readjusting my teaching for the year."

Indeed, if you don't get the results until the summer, you probably won't be able to meet with the teacher to discuss your child's scores or be directly involved in any decisions the school makes about your child based on the test scores. And even if you do get the results toward the end of the year, all those months in which your child might have benefited from enrichment or remedial help are lost. Unfortunately, this is often the best that your school can do. Make sure, however, that the bureaucratic bottleneck isn't happening at the school end of the reporting process.

School, District, and State Policy on Test Scores

Following each testing season, every state and many districts compile school or district "report cards," based on average student scores by grade, school, and district. These reports are released by the state or district to media outlets. These days, the information often goes straight to the World Wide Web; in fact, larger school districts often post average scores on their own web site. The public attention is welcomed by schools who can boast superior scores and embarrassing for those who do less well. The increasingly fierce test-score competition between schools is sure to have a growing impact on your school's curriculum and testing program.

Your Child's Test Results and National Education Goals

Goals 2000, perhaps the most prominent of recent national education initiatives, was created in 1991 by the Bush Administration, championed by the Clinton Administration, and widely adopted across the country. One major goal, for example, is that "U.S. students will be first in the world in science by the year 2000." This public agenda for educational excellence, it is hoped, will spur competition and encourage teachers, schools, and districts to focus more energy on improving science instruction and learning. The Goals initiative and subsequent legislation have inspired states to adopt curriculum standards that describe, year by year, what students will study in each subject area. The availability of clearly defined standards helps parents feel that their children are learning what is required for promotion from grade to grade.

The adoption of national goals, say its supporters, will also ensure that schools throughout the country maintain equivalent minimum levels of instructional quality; all students will be taught the same standards that will be assessed by standardized tests.

An additional aspect of this initiative is a commitment to test U.S. students each year to see how well the nation's students in general are progressing toward this goal. The TIMSS (Third International Math and Science Study) and NAEP (National Assessment of Educational Progress) testing programs are two national tests that already do this.

WHEN THE RESULTS ARE SURPRISING

Because schools look at test results chiefly to measure the performance of the student body as a whole, you may have to take the lead in getting the school to pay attention to your own child's test results.

Should you? Not always. It is usually unnecessary to have these discussions when your child's tests results are what you expected them to be and in line with past performance. The main reason to have the school focus on your child's test scores is when they deviate substantially from the general pattern of his school work. Because standardized tests are independent and objective, they may give you just the evidence you need to pursue a remedial program or an enrichment program for your child, as called for.

Let's examine a few common scenarios where the test scores are surprising.

My Child Did Poorly

Quiet, please. We're eavesdropping. This is the home of Edward and Angela Tarp. The kids have finally gone to sleep and now, sitting in the living room, the Tarps finally have a private moment together. Edward is waving his daughter Melissa's test scores in his hand. He is upset.

"Terrible. Just terrible. There's no point in sugar-coating it." Edward looks again at the numbers. "A 42 percentile in math. This is really disappointing. I've been telling you Melissa lacks a sense of responsibility for her work. You let her talk on the phone for hours and watch those idiotic TV shows. I'm sorry, but these scores are just unacceptable."

"What do you mean by 'unacceptable'?" Angela asks, genuinely curious but also signaling that she doesn't agree with her husband's gloomy assessment, nor does she appreciate being put on the defensive. "What's so terrible? From what I can tell, 42% is pretty close to average. And, in fact, Melissa works as hard as anyone else in her class. I don't know what you want from the girl."

As this evening's soap opera continues, Melissa's test scores become a touchstone for other intricate interactions between the couple. This isn't unusual: parents have a personal investment in their child's test scores that goes beyond the immediate relevance of the scores themselves. Reactions can become especially over-wrought when a child brings home low marks. In these circum-stances, it is particularly important to gain perspective, put your egos on hold, and refocus on what matters most here—your child's future.

What does it mean to have done poorly on a standardized test? There are two ways of defining this:

a) Melissa's scores were significantly lower than her grade level in one or more subjects

b) Melissa did significantly worse than expected based on her past performance

Let's take a look at the first definition. Suppose Melissa has been having a less than stellar year in the fourth grade. She has not done well on her school tests. She's been distant in the classroom and rarely raises her hand to contribute to the class discussion. She's lax about doing homework and when she does, the results are invari-ably sloppy and hurried. She rarely reads of her own volition. Clearly, Melissa is not working up to her grade level.

In this situation, her low scores on the standardized test are hardly surprising; they fit within the pattern of her general school work. Melissa's parents should view these scores as further, inde-pendent evidence that she needs to improve her studies. As a first step, they should address several key questions. Are Melissa's prob-lems cognitive—does she have the ability to learn this material? Are the problems attitudinal—does she have undetected emotional dif-ficulties that impede her learning? Are the problems organiza-tional—does Melissa need help with her study habits?

Parents can't answer these questions by themselves. They need to explore these issues with the child's teacher and school specialists and work together to solve what problems exist.

In the second definition of "did terribly," we are measuring Melissa's test scores against her own past performance. Suppose Melissa is an excellent student who regularly does well on her classroom exams and standardized tests. Her recent scores, then, are an anomaly, a deviation from her normal high level of achievement. The response required here is different from the one above.

First, her parents should bear in mind that everyone can have a bad day, and perhaps the best thing to do is simply ignore the results for now. More generally, Melissa may have problems with the new forms of standardized tests. If so, the problem can be remedied by targeting the nature of the difficulty—say, newly developed anxiety or a lack of requisite test-taking skill.

A more potent and urgent possibility is that the disappointing test result uncovered a genuine deficiency in Melissa's learning facilities. One of the chief attributes of a well-designed standardized test is its ability to pinpoint specific problems—in math computation, for example, or reading comprehension—that might otherwise go unnoticed in class. If Melissa's parents suspect that this may be the case, they should discuss this with her teacher, who will now look for other evidence of this gap in her learning skills.

The teacher may, as a result, recommend that Melissa undergo further testing to see if the problem is genuine. Educational experts, you'll be pleased to know, have become markedly sophisticated at precision targeting of learning deficiencies and have developed a variety of effective techniques for helping students overcome their learning inadequacies.

My Child Did Great

This is the flip side of the earlier scenario, but of course this time the parental mood is one of gloating rather than dismay. But here, too, the potential is rife for counterproductive self-deception.

As before, we need to be clear what we mean in saying that a child did superbly on a standardized test. Do we mean compared with other students in her grade or in contrast to our expectations?

If your child scores extremely well on his standardized tests and does well in his in-class exams, hands in his work on time, participates in classroom activities, loves to read, and is interested in new ideas, these standardized test results are just further confirmation that your child is flourishing. Keep doing whatever you're doing.

If, on the other hand, your child has scored unexpectedly high, this may be an indication that he has been systematically underachieving. If so, why, in fact, is this happening? Is your child bored in school? Is he having neglected emotional problems? Difficulties with the teacher or his classmates? Is stress in your home life contributing to his poor school work? Are you providing an intellectually engaging environment?

Arrange to discuss these possibilities with your child's teacher. Neither you nor your teacher can make this determination by yourselves—this must be a joint effort.

THE TEST RESULTS: WHOSE BUSINESS IS IT ANYWAY?

"Hey whatdja get on the test?"
No matter what, kids will talk about their grades with their friends, their would-be friends, and their current enemies. Showing off is a hallowed human trait, and so is the search for sympathy—but this response is especially entrenched when it comes to grades. The habit is bred early, instigated, in fact, by teachers. Do you remember how they'd hang the best papers on the wall for the collective admiration of the class? Little Johnny preened when his work decorated the classroom bulletin board while the rest of the class sulked at their own neglect.

Parents these days have become active participants in grade bragging-rights. Take a trip to any American shopping mall and you're likely to see more than a few cars with bumper stickers proclaiming, "My child is an honor student at (your local school name goes here)." Other parents, their hackles raised, exhibit stickers that read, "My child beat up your honor student." This sticker war reflects a deep-seated unease and equivocation about grades. Our children's behavior reflects that tension.

Should you discourage your child from discussing his test results with his peers? Probably. First, most children, particularly in younger grades, don't understand what these results really signify. They know what it means to get an 86 on their classroom history test, but an 86th percentile on a norm-referenced standardized test isn't the same thing—it's not about getting 86 percent of the questions right. In general, children don't appreciate the complex measurements and interpretations of criterion- and norm-referenced tests.

> *I have never let my schooling interfere with my education.*
> *—Mark Twain*

This is your call. Standardized test results are almost always sent directly to the parents from the school. They are not posted in the classroom or handed to the children. (If a teacher does announce grades to the class, you should complain and see that this procedure is abolished.) It is you who will tell the child how he or she did on the exam, and it is extremely important that you relay this information sensibly and with sensitivity.

You should, as a rule, tell your child, if only in broad strokes, how he did. This way the child can connect the test with outcomes; test-taking is usually not much fun, so it's important that he see how the test provides useful information about his learning skills. Moreover, after telling your child about his performance on the exam, you can now have a practical discussion about his strengths and weaknesses and what should be done to improve his education. If remedial or enrichment classes are in order, your child will now have a better understanding of the reasons for this decision. Make sure, however, that you have this conversation only after you yourself have become thoroughly familiar with the test results and have read through all the explanatory material that accompanies the scores.

How you communicate the results to your child—your choice of words, your tone, your gestures—can have a profound and lasting impact on your child's psyche. Children are at the age when identities are formed and are especially open to labeling. They are forming critical self-ascriptions of themselves as bright or laggards, clever or dull, superior test-takers or deficient test-takers. Telling a child who scored well, "Hey Carry, did you know that you are smarter than 94% of other American kids," not only distorts the meaning of the test results but also distorts your child's self-understanding; you also unfairly set her up for future disappointment. The parent who says to the child with a low score, "Barry, your math score was awful. You're really an inferior math student" goes a long way to ensuring that Barry will remain a poor math student.

Put the test results in context. Make sure your child understands that this is only a single test and that no permanent generalizations can be inferred from the result. Ask your child whether she thinks the results reflect her true ability. If her scores were significantly below standard, ask her if she'd like more help; if significantly better than the norm, ask if she'd like more enrichment. Make sure your child doesn't perceive you as a judge reading out a sentence but as a caring parent who wants to use the results as a springboard for further discussion. You know your child, and you know better than anyone how you can do this most effectively.

Chapter 7

You and Your Child's Teacher

Beth Osten, a fourth grade teacher in St. Paul, Minnesota, says she expects to deal with at least one set of blustering parents a few days before a standardized test. "Typically, these are parents I haven't heard from all year long. They show up late to the parent-teacher conference, mostly to complain without bothering to listen and then I'll hear nothing from them.

"Now they're here to find out what I'm doing to help their child prepare for the test. To tell you the truth, I'm not inclined to give them more than a routine answer. It's not like I have this ongoing relationship with them. I'm thinking, 'If they're so concerned about their child's education, where have they been all year long?'"

Talking to your child's teacher about an upcoming standardized test can, in fact, be beneficial, but don't wait until the morning of the exam to introduce yourself to your child's teacher. Positive cooperation between parent and teacher needs cultivation and requires forethought and sensitivity. Sometimes, parents do more harm than good when they micro-manage their children's schooling and create unnecessary conflicts with school administrators and teachers. Here, then, are some suggestions on how to achieve this fruitful relationship.

GET TO KNOW YOUR CHILD'S TEACHER

The sooner you establish this dialogue, the better. One immediate consequence of your reaching out to make contact is that it indicates to the teacher that you are a parent who actively participates in her child's education. For example, the beginning of the school year is an excellent opportunity to review any special needs your child might have; teachers are incredibly busy at this time and may not have had a chance to review in detail the records of all their new students.

According to a recent Time/CNN survey, nearly 90 percent of the American public believe that lack of support from parents is a serious problem for public school teachers today.

With a healthy rapport in place, parents are more comfortable notifying their teacher about developments in the child's family life or reporting changes in their child's behavior. With an ever-heavy work load on their shoulders, even the best-intentioned teachers can miss something important happening to a student. Here is a not uncommon example.

A teacher in Downey, California, relates that it was more than a month before she learned that a child in her class had been diagnosed with a chronic bladder infection. During this period, the child was too embarrassed to ask for permission to go the bathroom and sat in extreme discomfort until it was time for recess. Once the teacher knew of his condition, she and the child devised a "secret code" that he could use to signal that he wanted to go to the bathroom. Just knowing he could do this eased the child's anxiety and allowed him to concentrate on his school work. Had the parent had an open relationship with the teacher, a month of under-achievement and discomfort could have been avoided.

GET THE MOST OUT OF PARENT-TEACHER CONFERENCES

The parent-teacher conference offers a unique opportunity to sit together for an uninterrupted period of time to review your child's educational progress and jointly develop strategies to improve your child's educational skills. Teachers complain that these sessions all too often are frittered away in unproductive chitchat. Here are some things you can do to accomplish more at these meetings:

- ◆ Save time by jotting down questions and concerns before the meeting.
- ◆ Be prepared, attitudinally as well as intellectually, to listen as well as to talk.
- ◆ Take notes to help you remember what was discussed during the conference.
- ◆ Ask for clarification when you don't understand something.
- ◆ Find out how grades are formulated and how you can improve your child's academic performance.
- ◆ Discuss specific ways you can help your child prepare for standardized tests.

GET INVOLVED WITH THE EDUCATIONAL PROCESS

Even if you work full-time, contribute to your child's educational environment. Your efforts will not only help improve the quality of education at your child's school, but will also demonstrate to your child that her education means a great deal to you. Again, there are several things you can do, in and out of the classroom, to help.

Offer to assist your child's teacher. Offer, don't demand. Allow the teacher to take the lead on how you can best contribute; some are more inclined to embrace parental help than others. Don't insist on only the glorious tasks—be willing to do the little things as well: prepare artwork, assemble bulletin boards, read to children, drill math facts. Incidentally, you needn't be too concerned that your presence in the classroom will distract your child. Most teachers report that the children of classroom helpers are better behaved than the rest of the class. You'll find out quickly enough if this doesn't turn out to be true in your case.

Parents can also help their child's class from home. You can, for example, assemble materials for art projects, help grade math papers, or assist in arranging class trips. When you "do homework" of this kind, the value you place in education has a significant impact on your child.

The child is the most avid learner of all living things on earth.
—Ashley Montague

On occasion, you might also undertake projects for the school and the wider community: help with school registration, work the book fair, tutor in the after-school program, and, if you're any good at it, by all means bake for the bake sale. Children notice this sort of parental commitment, and it does make a difference in their own attitudes.

In short: talk to your child's teacher early and often. Ask how you can help. And do it.

Chapter 8

◆

Children with Special Needs

Millions of children in the United States have serious learning difficulties. These students are no less entitled to an education than any other children. The Individuals with Disabilities Education Act, known as IDEA, makes those rights explicit. By law, learning-disabled children must be provided with a free public education that meets their individual special needs. These requirements include accommodations for standardized tests.

However—and this is a critical point—your child will *not* qualify for special consideration with regard to standardized tests unless he or she has first been diagnosed as learning disabled by the school's IEP, or Individualized Education Program. (More on the IEP later.)

You cannot show up the day before a standardized test and tell the teacher that, in fairness, your child should get extra time for the test because he has difficulty concentrating. You need to have noted this earlier and have had your child "officially" recognized as learning impaired.

As a parent of a learning-disabled child—or a child whom you suspect might have learning disabilities—you have several important questions to ask and answer:

- How do I determine if my child has a learning difficulty?
- Does my child have a problem that requires special arrangements for taking standardized tests?
- Who makes this determination?
- What can I do to help my learning-impeded child prepare for a standardized test?

As noted, not all children with learning problems are automatically exempt from taking standardized tests; not all even qualify for special test conditions. Before any such decision is made, the school must first establish that the child suffers from an inability that interferes with learning and test-taking. The criteria for such a decision are fairly well defined and exclude what might otherwise seem to some as a genuine learning obstacle. A child who hates school, refuses to do her homework, and requires the state militia to get her to go to class each morning is clearly having a difficult time with her education. A lack of motivation, however serious, does not qualify for special treatment when it comes to standardized tests.

But, before looking at specific learning disabilities and their consequences for standardized tests, it would be beneficial first to examine the broader issue of learning disabilities and school education.

WHAT IS A LEARNING DISABILITY?

Although our focus in this book is standardized testing, the concern with learning disabilities is, of course, much broader. At stake isn't just a child's performance on some exam, but the progress of his or her educational development and psychological health. Every parent should pay careful attention if they notice in their child a pattern of learning failures.

Many parents are inclined to point to a child's low score on a standardized test as compelling evidence that their child is "learning disabled." The reality, however, is that some children are simply not academic stars. On the other hand, if you have reason to believe that your child is genuinely bright and her scores nowhere reflect that intelligence, then a low score on standardized tests should definitely motivate you to try to explain the discrepancy. We have seen this happen often: parents discover that their children are learning disabled as a result of being upset by a poor performance on a standardized test.

This is waiting too long. You should begin the diagnostic process *before* the test, not after. Of course, you need to know what to look for—learning disabilities encompass deficiencies in every step of the learning process, from the intake of information to the storing and retrieving of information. And these obstacles can show up anywhere within the spectrum of educational skills: reading, writing, speaking, and mathematics.

THE GAP BETWEEN POTENTIAL AND PERFORMANCE

According to some recent estimates, 15-20 percent of American schoolchildren suffer from a serious learning adversity. Many parents are unaware that learning-disabled children are, as a rule, neither lazy nor academically slow. What these children share is a measurable gap between potential and performance. Because the learning process is so extraordinarily complex, structural flaws in assimilating information are subtle and can hide behind other learning successes. As a result, many children go through school without ever having their hardship detected.

Learning-disabled students often present a puzzle to their teachers—the child does outstanding work in one aspect of his school work and poorly in another. He might, for example, excel as a reader yet have enormous difficulty in writing. He might absorb information rapidly but struggle to recall that information. Or, though clearly intelligent, he might have enormous trouble concentrating and become frantic when asked to "stay on task."

These children are at least as perplexed as anyone by their behavior, and the consequences of their frustration are palpable. Thirty-five percent of students identified with learning disabilities drop out of high school—twice the rate of other students. And this number includes learning-disabled students who have been appropriately diagnosed and have received the benefit of educational counseling. Students who go through school with unattended learning disabilities are even more prone to feel bewildered and angry and often become intractable discipline problems at school and at home.

The responsibility is clear: If you have any reason at all to believe that your child might be suffering from a learning disability, it is your obligation as a parent to find out what that problem is and what you can do about it. An upcoming standardized test might be just the catalyst to get you moving.

Some Early Warning Signs

The key to successful help, as with all afflictions, is early intervention. As the child's parent, you—along with your child's teacher—are in the best position to notice peculiarities in the way your child is learning. Here are some telltale clues that might call for diagnostic testing:

- ◆ Letter or number reversal. This is a common mistake among preschoolers and kindergarten children. But if the problem persists in first grade and beyond, a parent should bring the difficulty to the teacher's attention (a competent teacher will probably already have noticed the tendency). Also worrisome is the habit of reversing letters left to right or up and down. Another, related symptom is the constant omission of a word or letter when reading.
- ◆ An inability to concentrate. Constant fidgeting, darting from topic to topic.

♦ Difficulties with following written or verbal instructions, poor motor coordination, and severely illegible handwriting.

THE ALL-IMPORTANT IEP

Every school is mandated to diagnose learning disabilities in their student population. The process is known as the Individualized Education Program, or IEP. The typical procedure is as follows. A battery of tests is administered to your child. An evaluation meeting is then scheduled with the participation of a Special Ed(ucation) professional, a teacher, and the child's parents; when appropriate, the child, too, might be present for part of the meeting. A determination is made about the best educational program for the child, and this plan then becomes your child's "IEP." The results are usually carefully reevaluated after the first year and every three years thereafter.

Once the evaluation is complete, you should ask the school for a parent consent form. This confirms in writing that you understand the school's evaluation and the decision to place your child in the designated educational program. You should make sure that the plan is in fact implemented as proposed and notify the school authorities if it is not. Take note, too, that if you do not agree with the school's decision, you have recourse to an independent professional psychologist who can undertake an unbiased evaluation of your child.

The IEP and Standardized Tests

This is worth repeating: Your child will not qualify for special consideration with regard to standardized tests unless he or she has first been diagnosed as being learning disabled by the school's IEP. Children who are designated by the IEP as learning disabled will often qualify to take their standardized tests in special settings. In some cases, they will be exempt from the test, or part of it, entirely. For example, a dyslexic child may be required to take the math sections of a standardized test but not the verbal sections. Other learning-impaired children may be given untimed or extended-time tests, be granted extra breaks during the test, or have the test administered to them in small groups.

In general, the current trend is to allow learning-disabled students to take standardized tests in the same way they take their other classroom tests. Such special test settings may mean taking the test alone, in a Special-Ed classroom, or even at home. Responses may be communicated differently, in sign language or by pointing to the right answer. And, as noted, time requirements may be suitably reconfigured.

A final reminder: If your child will be taking a standardized test, review with the teacher what special arrangements will be put in place. If you aren't sure whether your child has been designated as learning disabled, ask. And if you don't get an answer, look it up in your child's IEP in his school file—you are legally required to be given access to these forms.

PREPARING FOR A STANDARDIZED TEST: A GUIDE FOR LEARNING-DISABLED STUDENTS

Because the term "learning disabled" is a catch-all phrase for a wide variety of learning impediments, any discussion of test preparation for this population needs to address *specific* difficulties. Different strategies work well for some kinds of impairments, but not for others. Here, then, is a closer look at the more common learning disabilities and at how parents can help these children prepare for standardized tests.

THE DYSLEXIC CHILD

There is no standard definition of dyslexia. The more expansive definitions of the word include most reading disorders, but some educators prefer to restrict the term to a reading dysfunction in which one systematically reverses numbers or letters, perceives letters or numbers upside down, or reverses word order—for example, reading "was" for "saw."

In any case, dyslexic children have demonstrable difficulties with one or more aspects of language: listening, speaking, spelling, writing, and reading. In fact, reading problems are the most common of all learning disabilities and often the most debilitating—reading, after all, is at the heart of learning.

When these inabilities are left unattended, the inevitable result is a shortchanged education. The emotional fallout is also considerable. Dyslexic children find the process of reading grueling, emotionally draining, and embarrassing. They are constantly struggling to make sense of letters and words that persist in dancing, wriggling, and darting across the page. Children with dyslexia often lose their self-confidence and come to feel inadequate.

A parent who suspects that his child might be dyslexic should immediately have the child tested and help develop an educational program tailored to the child's needs.

Dyslexia and Standardized Tests

As one might expect, dyslexic children face special difficulties in taking standardized tests. These tests demand competent reading skills, which dyslexics lack. The time pressure and rigid test settings only add to the child's anxieties. There are, however, a few helpful things that parents can do.

First, considerable progress is being made in treating dyslexic children, so seek out the best professional help. Among the various methods currently used to treat dyslexia are:

- ◆ Visual tracking exercises (workbooks and other remedial materials)
- ◆ Multi-sensory instruction packages and programs
- ◆ Eye muscle training and other developmental optometric exercises

Learn how you can employ these techniques when you are alone with your child.

There are also a number of steps you can take specifically in preparing for standardized tests:

◆ *Talk to your school's resource specialist.* Find out what testing accommodations are available for your child. And make sure that they are implemented before the test begins.

◆ *Encourage your child.* Dyslexic children have painful associations with reading. You need to overcome these responses if your child is to take a standardized test. Try to make reading a positive experience while being sensitive to your child's feelings of disappointment and inadequacy.

◆ *Build your child's confidence.* For example, find books that she finds especially interesting but are somewhat below her reading level. A successful reading venture will help her feel positive about her self and her reading abilities.

ADD and ADHD

During the past several years, many children have been diagnosed with Attention Deficit Disorder (ADD) and Attention Deficit Hyperactivity Disorder (ADHD). According to current estimates, between two and four percent of all children suffer from these disorders. As with most learning disabilities, children who have this affliction are, on average, no less intelligent than the rest of the population; indeed, on the basis of their autobiographical comments and descriptions of their behavioral patterns, it is now believed that such luminaries as Thomas Edison and Benjamin Franklin suffered from ADD.

Technically, ADD and ADHD are not considered learning disabilities, although children with these disorders may suffer from other learning impairments and should be given a comprehensive assessment exam to find out if this is the case.

If your child has been diagnosed as ADD or ADHD, it is important that you understand how this can affect his education generally and his performance on standardized tests in particular.

What Are ADD and ADHD?

First, some definitions. ADD and ADHD are similar disorders. Children who suffer from these syndromes share the symptoms of "distractibility and impulsivity." They find it difficult to sit still in class and pay attention to the teacher. Instead, they stare out the window at the birds or fix their attention on a fly buzzing in the room and are easily irritated by the fidgeting of the child nearby.

In a sense, rather than lacking attentiveness, these children can be described as overly attentive, responding to all the stimuli in their environment. This disposition makes it nearly impossible to concentrate on any one task for a sustained period of time.

The dominant symptom of ADD is "hypo-activity," or listlessness, while children with ADHD characteristically manifest an over-abundance of energy. Children with ADHD will not only stare out the window but will rock in their chairs while doing so, kick their feet about, and, perhaps, periodically leap out of their chairs. These hyperactive children have extremely brief attention spans and are often disruptive in classroom settings.

Whereas children with ADD tend to be daydreamers, passive and lethargic, and appear to be lazy and uninterested, children with ADHD are generally intense, restless, and over-reactive and appear to be nervous and "jumpy."

ADD, ADHD, and Standardized Tests

If you child suffers from ADD or ADHD, he is likely to have problems both preparing for and taking standardized tests. The first set of obstacles are social. Children with these disorders are given to angry outbursts and are quick to get into fights and blame others for their shortcomings. They are also highly sensitive to criticism. This makes test preparation especially volatile—pointing out wrong answers, for example, can easily be taken as a personal rebuke by the child.

Standardized tests confront the ADD or ADHD child with a set of significant hurdles that need to be carefully addressed. These

Behold the Turtle:
He makes progress only
when he stick his neck out.
—James O. Conant

tests demand sustained attention to details, a huge barrier for children with this disorder. Standardized tests require attending to the task at hand for an extended period, also a difficult challenge for children who constantly flit from one item to another. Likewise, verbal directions are important in standardized tests, and this can be a significant pitfall for children who tend to "zone out" when given directions. Individuals with ADD or ADHD also have problems dealing with repeated patterns, and standardized tests often demand that one do the same sort of task again and again.

What Can You Do To Help?

As always, the first step is early diagnosis. As soon as a parent has an inkling or suspicion that her child might be suffering from this disorder, she should have him examined. The standard treatment for ADD and ADHD is Ritalin, a drug already in use for several decades that usually provides substantial benefits and whose side-effects are minimal and well documented.

In helping an ADD/ADHD child prepare for a standardized test, the key is to address the specific behavioral attributes of this disorder. First and certainly foremost, make certain that your child is aware of what to expect in a standardized test. He should be ready for the challenge of focusing on a problem and learn how to resist the temptation to dart from one problem to the next. It might help to have him ask himself, "Why am I giving in to this temptation? Don't I want to answer this question?" This "self-talk" has proved useful for many with ADD and ADHD.

To succeed at standardized tests, an understanding of the directions is crucial. Because children with ADD and ADHD find it hard to follow directions, they need to practice this skill. They need to learn how to become active listeners. Having them repeat what they have heard is one technique that sometimes helps improve the assimilation of directions.

Finally, do practice tests with your child. Start slowly and build up his attention span. Knowing what to expect will ease his surprise and reduce anxiety at test time.

PHYSICAL DISABILITIES

Children with physical disabilities do not automatically qualify for special testing conditions. Their IEPs will not call for special accommodations unless their disability is found to interfere with their ability to learn and to take tests. In some cases, the physical hardship clearly does not present obstacles to learning—a child who uses a cane but is otherwise in good physical health does not need special consideration in taking standardized tests.

On the other hand, some physical disabilities, such as significantly diminished hearing or sight, limited gross and fine motor skills, muscular diseases, head traumas, and spinal injuries, clearly do impede learning and taking exams. If your child has a physical disability that you believe makes it difficult for her to take a standardized test in normal settings under routine constraints, make sure to discuss this with the teacher and work out an arrangement that is suitable for your child.

Remember: Your child has a legally mandated right to special accommodations in the school setting. For example, if he is hearing impaired, he has the right to have an interpreter with him during the test. Similarly, to help children with limited or no vision, Harcourt Brace, for example, publishes its widely used Stanford 9 standardized test in both Braille and in large print. Again, make sure you are familiar with the special arrangements recommended by your child's IEP and review those procedures with your child's teacher.

THE BILINGUAL STUDENT

Bilingual education is currently one of the nation's most controversial issues. Our immediate concern, however, is not with educational policy but with how parents can best help children for whom English is not their native tongue do well on standardized tests.

◆

In 1997, the number of children in the United States who were either immigrants or American-born children of immigrants was 13.7 million, up from 8 million in 1990. This group comprises the fastest-growing segment of the U.S. population under 18 years of age.

◆

This is hardly an uncommon problem. Nearly three million children in the United States either do not speak English as their first language or lack a functional knowledge of English. This number is expected to double in the next 20 years.

Bilingual programs are most often implemented in urban schools. Students in suburban and rural districts whose first language is not English are usually taught the language as part of an ESL, or English as a Second Language, program. These ESL classes are designed to supplement the regular curriculum.

Bilingual Students and Standardized Tests

Some states exclude students who are not fluent English speakers from state assessment programs. In most instances, the guidelines are specific and unequivocal. Typically, whether a state includes LEP (or Limited English Speaking) students in their standardized tests depends on how long a student has been in the country or in an ESL program and on how well he has scored on English proficiency tests. Currently, 38 states permit exemptions of LEP students from all or part of their standardized tests.

Because policies differ considerably from state to state, it is imperative that you check with your school to see if your child will be exempted from standardized tests. California, for example, requires all LEP students to take the English version of the Stanford

9 standardized test, even if they do not speak a word of English. Make sure, too, to find out whether your child will be asked to take a test in her own first language.

EL ESTUDIANTE BILINGÜE

La educación bilingüe es una de los temas más discutidos del país. Nuestra preocupación, sin embargo, no es con la política educativa, sino con la manera en que los padres pueden ayudar a los niños para los cuales el inglés no es su primer idioma, salir bien en los exámenes estandardizados.

Esta no es una preocupación aislada. Casi tres milliones de niños en los Estados Unidos o no hablan inglés como su primer idioma o no tienen un entendimiento funcional del inglés. Se espera que este número se duplique en los próximos veinte años.

Los programas bilingües estan implementados más frequentemente en las escuelas urbanizados. Los estudiantes en distritos suburbanos y rurales cuyo primer idioma no es inglés normalmente aprenden el lenguaje como parte del programa ESL, o "English as a Second Language" [Inglés Como Segundo Idioma]. Estas clases son diseñadas para suplementar el programa regular.

En 1997, el número de niños imigrantes o hijos nacidos en America a imigrantes en los Estados Unidos fue 13.7 milliones, comparado a 8 milliones en 1990. Este grupo es el segmento de crecimiento mas rápido de la población de los Estados Unidos menor de 18 años de edad.

Los Estudiantes Bilingües y Los Exámenes Estandardizados

Algunos estados excluyen a los estudiantes que no hablan inglés con fluencia de los programas de evaluación del estado. En la mayoría de los casos, las guías son específicas e inflexibles. Tipicamente, si un estado permite estudiantes LEP, o "Limited English Speaking"

[Hablar Inglés con Límites], tomar exámenes estandardizados depende de cuanto tiempo el estudiante ha estado en el país, o en un programa ESL, y en las buenas notas en los exámenes de adelanto en inglés. Corrientemente, 38 estados permiten exenciones a estudiantes LEP de todo o parte de los exámenes estandardizados.

Porque las reglas son considerablemente diferentes de un estado a otro, es imperativo que usted chequee con su escuela para ver si su hijo va a ser eximido de los exámenes estandardizados. California, por ejemplo, requiere que todos los estudiantes LEP tomen la versión inglés del examen estandardizado que se llama Stanford 9, aunque no hablen ni una palabra de inglés. Averigue, además, si su hijo tendrá que tomar un examen en su propio idioma.

Chapter 9

◆

The Real Test Is In Your Home

You're concerned about your child's upcoming standardized test, and that makes sense. But let's keep our eye on the real prize. You're in this for the long haul. Your child will take standardized tests not just this year, but the year to follow and years after that, straight through high school. But not even the entire range of these exams is the ultimate target here. What matters, finally, is *all* of your child's education. Your aim is to prepare your children for lifelong learning by planting their educational roots in your home. This isn't just vacuous rhetoric . . . it's a central obligation—and satisfaction—of parenthood.

Study after study confirms what we all intuitively recognize: parental involvement contributes significantly to student performance. For example, a recent in-depth study conducted by the National Committee for Citizens in Education showed that children whose parents were actively involved in their education scored higher on tests, were better behaved in class, were more conscientious, and continued to perform better academically years later.

We don't want to get sidetracked here into the ongoing debate over the quality of our nation's schools—as it is, we spend much of our professional lives in the crossfire of that dispute. But one thing is clear: involvement in your children's education is more crucial now than ever.

Parents no longer have the luxury of assuming that the school will do all the educating and will be the chief institution that shapes the thinking processes of children. The reality is that children get bombarded with more information out of school than in. The onslaught comes at them in the form of advertising, television shows, movies, the Internet, music, and magazines. The messages are loud, intense, and demanding, and they're underscored by peer-group pressure. An intense competition is underway for your child's attention, and you are in charge of monitoring that contest and deciding who has access to your child's mind. For make no mistake: all those unsupervised hours of a child's day are filled by the marketplace. You may not be happy with the results.

A final word in this introductory sermonette. We all have our justifiable excuses. Most American parents work, both fathers and mothers. We have too few hours to spend with our kids. But this is all the more reason, not less, to enrich those hours, to take control, and to make your time together with your child fun and fulfilling for all.

Okay, then. Here our some ideas on how to turn your home into a productive learning environment.

MAKE LEARNING FUN AGAIN

Do you remember how incredibly smart your child was as a baby? How much information she soaked up before she went to school? Indeed, two- and three-year-olds are linguistic geniuses; in the space of several months, they progress from knowing 30 words to knowing thousands, and they somehow learn to construct sentences that astonish you in their complexity. Had your child grown up in a home where three languages were spoken, she'd be adept at all three. In her pre-school years, your child learned to count, to identify all sorts of objects in her world, to sing and to dance.

None of this was "work." Curiosity is natural to children. Gathering new information was a delight for your child and a delight for you to observe and assist. Alas, your child then went to school, and learning became "schoolwork," a day full of assignments and burdensome obligations. The pure fun of discovery disappeared.

Indeed, whoever coined the word "homework" performed a great disservice to humankind. Who the heck wants to come home to do "work"? Do you? Had we called after-school assignments "homeplay" or even "home-learning," children would be more eager to further their day's studies. You can help change that mindset about learning at home by making learning fun again.

It's easier than you think. Rid yourself of the notion that creating a learning environment in the home is an onus on your children. The pleasure will be theirs. Your child's inherent curiosity about new information is still alive, ready, and willing. Properly challenged, he will enjoy the adventure of learning more than playing Sega for the fortieth time this evening.

THE PUNISHING EFFECT OF REWARDS

A school district in the Midwest had a bright idea about how to get the kids in school to read more. They'd offer free pizza to any child who read 10 books or more over a period of a few months. Some kids did get the free pizza—and disdained reading as a result.

Much of our educational research just confirms the obvious, as do those studies on the importance of parental involvement. But sometimes research in developmental psychology reveals surprising conclusions. One such counter-intuitive finding is that rewards are bad for children.

Let's hasten to qualify this sweeping statement. Obviously, not all rewards are deleterious to a child's education. Nonetheless, the basic thrust of this claim is supported by mountains of evidence. Rewarding children for learning tends to undermine their interest in learning.

Our educational system and our parenting styles routinely rely on what psychologists call "extrinsic motivation." We give stickers to pre-schoolers for their pretty drawings and distribute stars and certificates thereafter for their good work. The second half of extrinsic motivation is punishment. We threaten to deprive children of their expected goodies if they don't perform as they should. But external motivation, both positive and negative, is ineffective over the long run.

Here's an example. Getting your child to practice the piano is a battle in most homes. But as your child becomes skilled at the instrument, the real motivation to practice comes from the music itself. The ability to play is self-rewarding. Psychologists call this "intrinsic motivation," and it is a much stronger incentive than outside pressure. Giving a child money to practice only turns the joy of playing music into a chore, like mowing the lawn. It saps the joy and undermines desire. That was the effect of the Midwestern school district's reading bribe. The children who wanted the pizza read just the 10 books—the slimmest, easiest books they could get their hands on—and then stopped reading as soon as they got their free pizza. A more effective campaign would have offered free books to all children who ate 10 pizzas—this way, reading would be the valued prize, not pizza. (Mark Twain understood this principle. Remember how Tom Sawyer got his friends to paint his fence for him by making them pay for the privilege?)

The worthwhile learning activities you develop for your child will be self-reinforcing. A bit of "extrinsic motivation" might help at the beginning to get them started, but only a bit. Trust in the joy of satisfying our natural human curiosity and the pleasures of self-motivated learning.

> *Understanding physics is child's play compared to understanding child's play.*
> —*Albert Einstein*

MAKE READING #1 IN YOUR HOME

All standardized tests require reading skills. Even math and science tests have verbal problems. The formula is unequivocal: To succeed on standardized tests, in classroom tests, in school in general, indeed in life, you need good reading skills. And home is where these skills are nurtured.

Nothing creates an interest in reading like reading itself. Parents can help children develop the reading habit by making this a daily activity. From the first grade on, your child should read *every single day*. What a child reads matters far less than that he or she reads. A magazine article about fashion, music, sports, celebrities—the time a child devotes to reading is almost always time better spent than doing nearly anything else. Reading directly improves a child's vocabulary and reading comprehension, increases her stock of information, and sharpens her critical thinking.

Here's a guarantee. Reading will improve all these skills and, as a result, improve your child's scores on standardized tests.

Why will your child sit down every evening to read? Because you will. Some educators suggest, and it's not a bad idea, to schedule D.E.A.R. time—as in, Drop Everything And Read. This blocked-out period—say, 20 minutes after dinner—is set aside for reading by everyone in the house. The television is off, the answering machine is on, and everyone reads. By participating in this activity, you demonstrate by example—the most effective way parents convey their convictions—how much you value reading.

You might also, when appropriate, read aloud with your child. This is a terrific way to communicate ideas and encourage conversation and discussion.

One more thing: don't be shy about getting help. Children are forever complaining, "Yeah, but there's nothing to read. The books we have in the house are so boring." There's an endless sea of captivating books to bring home. For starters, look for books on subjects that your child already has an interest in, whatever that interest happens to be—a biography of Michael Jordan, a book on how to make a movie, a history of dogs, a book on roller-blading, spooky stories, or a book on siblings if a new addition to the family is on the way. Ask your local librarian and local bookstore for suggestions.

And don't get too upset if your child seems stuck on reading frivolous books. Reading junk is like eating junk. We all enjoy an occasional meal at McDonald's, but few of us would choose to make those outings the staple of our diet. Similarly, with a little nudge from you and a few helpful suggestions, your child will seek out quality books on his own. Once he's savored better written material, reading junk will become as boring to him as eating junk food is to people with more sophisticated taste.

IT'S JUST A GAME

"Just" is not a *just* word in this context. Playing games and working on puzzles are superb ways to accumulate knowledge and develop cognitive skills—indeed, some learning theorists argue that all learning is akin to problem-solving. Puzzles can be found both in a department store's toy section and in the education and math sections of a bookstore. In one setting the activity is deemed "serious," and in the other it is play. The distinction is arbitrary.

Ask yourself: When did you and your child last spend a rainy day doing a jigsaw puzzle together? This is a wonderful way to develop analytical and spatial skills (and get to hang with each other too). "Brain-teasers" are an excellent—and entertaining—way to develop deductive thinking. Many excellent thinking-puzzle books are available at your bookstore, but you also might try to create puzzles of your own. These exercises in logical reasoning will translate into better grades in school as well as enhance your child's performance on standardized tests.

One word of caution though: Don't present puzzles as a test. That's a sure way to ruin any interest in solving them. Allow your child to address these posers in his own way and at his own pace. You're there as a coach, not a judge.

RE-CREATE RECREATION

The ancient Greek word for leisure is *scolia*, which means school. The word for work is *ascolia*, not school. For the ancient Greeks, true leisure was time devoted to learning and work was time that kept you from educating yourself. Very young children always learn as they play and so should older children—indeed, so should adults.

You can enhance the math skills of your children by, say, cooking with them. "Okay, James, how many cups are there in this quart? Sandy, we just need a third of the six eggs this recipe calls for—how many eggs do you think we'll use?" Cooking is also a great laboratory for learning science. "All right, smarties, can anyone guess why water boils more quickly if we put a lid on the pot?"

Sports is another recreational pass-time that can become more fruitful than just passing time. Many a young person has learned percentage by calculating batting averages and three-point shots. "So here's the question, Heather: Shaquille O'Neal just scored 11 points in the first quarter. If he keeps up the pace and scores the same amount in each of the remaining quarters, how many points will he score for the game?" (With an older child, you can up the stakes—and introduce the fine art of sports gambling: "Wanna bet a nickel that Shaq's first-quarter score is more than 40% of his game total?")

Travel time is always ripe learning time. "Hey, captain, could you please calculate how many miles we can go on this tank of gas?" Give your child a map and ask him to figure out the best route to your destination . . . and then (if it isn't too wacky) follow his route! Be innovative. Create exciting challenges for your child that are also opportunities to explore new ideas and sharpen thinking. He'll do

> *If families teach the love of learning, it can make all the difference in the world to their children.*
> —*Richard W. Riley, U.S. Secretary of Education*

better on standardized tests as a result because these sorts of questions are similar to those on the exams—and your child will already have mastered them in the ordinary course of play.

A SPACE OF HIS OWN

In our chapter on preparing for the test, we urged you to set aside a place for your child to study. In fact, this should be a permanent arrangement. Designating a study space for even a young child communicates the message that schoolwork is a top priority. After all, how important do you think your child feels about doing homework if you haven't provided a table or desk on which to work?

This space needn't be luxurious, but it ought to be quiet and comfortable and belong to your child for the express purpose of doing school assignments.

CAN WE TALK?

The U.S. Department of Education cites studies showing that frequent, open family discussions are associated with higher student achievement. A bevy of additional research indicates that even with standardized tests that target cognitive abilities, not factual content, the inventory of information students bring to the test contributes significantly to performance. You can help educate your children by making them more intelligent, and you can help make them more intelligent by talking to them.

Talk about the world you live in. Discuss current events. Your family history. Moral dilemmas, public and personal. Talk about your work and ask for suggestions. Talk about future aspirations and dreams. Discuss, argue, consider, reconsider, speculate, imagine, analyze. And listen. By really listening to your child, you show her that you respect and care about her ideas and feelings. You also demonstrate by example how critical good listening is to good conversation. So talk with your child—you might learn something.

THE LINE ON GETTING ON-LINE

More than a million and half computers were in operation in our schools in 1997. Thirty-eight percent of high school students now work on their own computers at home. In just a few years, computers will be as universal as radios, television sets, and VCRs. But there is this difference—in most homes, it is the children who explain the technology to the parents, who show them how to load an application or access a web site.

Children have mastered the rhetoric they need to cajole their parents into allowing them to spend hours playing games on their computers: "Hey mom, it's not passive like watching television. It's interactive." Parents respond with marked ambivalence, an uncertainty that reflects their confusion about the appropriate role of computers in their child's education. This is, after all, a new technology for most adults, so we have no personal experiences, no clear intuition, to guide us. Which way does caution lie? Do you encourage your child to do her homework on the computer and chat on-line and run the risk of her not learning basic skills or, alternatively, discourage her from spending time on the computer and run the risk of impeding her fluency in the medium of the future? You need to exercise intelligence and realism.

> *A good education is the next best thing to a pushy mother.*
> *—Charles Schulz*

Above all, don't be driven by your own ideological venting. Computers are an integral part of our children's life and education. And they do offer some extraordinary benefits (extraordinary, that is, to us adults).

For one thing, computers can help your child get organized. No longer does he need to have papers flying all over the house. Software writing programs can help your child edit his work and provide grammar and spelling checks. They also come with templates for outlining and the means for easily creating charts and graphs. All these skills help make your child a better student. This does not mean that you ought to throw away the family dictionary and encyclopedia, but it does mean that your insistence that only books be used as reference tools is probably no more than generational prejudice.

A number of excellent educational software programs are also available that can enhance your child's verbal and mathematical skills. Many students who otherwise would not submit to practicing their math tables, say, or bother reviewing the rules of conjugation in French are happy to learn and practice this material if it comes at them in the form of an entertaining challenge on the computer screen. Indeed, many companies publish CD-ROMs that help students build their academic skills and thereby prepare for standardized tests. To help guide you in this area, we've assembled a selective list of these educational products in Appendix C.

> *Too often, we give children answers to remember rather than problems to solve.*
> *—Roger Lewin*

What about the Internet? Going on-line opens up an entire new world for students. The resources for information are now dazzling—no wonder so many parents are dumfounded and suspicious. Like it or not, your daughter is not kidding when she says that, say, the Natural Museum provides her with precisely the information she needs for her report on Tyrannosaurus Rex. And she's telling you the truth, too, when she says there are specialists out there who will e-mail explanatory answers to the questions she has sent them. The social ramifications of chat-lines are a separate subject but we should note the positive educational potential in conversations with other children all over the globe. The more your child learns, the more curious she is to learn more—and the better she will do on standardized tests.

Computers have their downsides, of course. They can become receptacles for enormous wastes of time. Instead of downloading information for his paleontology report, your son might be spending hours playing mindless, addictive computer games. And those chat sessions might be no more than forays into pointless gossip.

In any case, this technology belongs to our children. They are usually better at it than their parents and more comfortable with the ongoing parade of technological improvements. Nonetheless, you are still the parent and it is your obligation to monitor and supervise both the time spent on the machine and the activities it is used for. Don't be daunted—if the technology is foreign to you, become familiar with it. You owe it to your child's education.

We should also emphasize the crucial importance of computer skills in standardized tests. In fact, many tests are already being administered via computer, and this will become routine in the years ahead. Developing your child's comfort with computing will become essential for test performance in the future. Get your child ready now.

TELEVISION: TACTICS FOR GETTING BY WITH A LITTLE

When it comes to television, here's the central statistic, the one that finally matters: by the time the average American is 18, he or she will have spent more time in front of the television than in the classroom. Any discussion about parental involvement in the education of their children must address television head-on, not as some side topic.

It's not enough to bemoan the influence of television on our children, hurl impassioned speeches about how the wasteland of television is wasting our children's energies, and wish it were otherwise. In fact, children spend countless hours watching television— 44 percent of seventh-graders recently reported watching three or more hours of television a day; the average school child watches an average of 27 hours a week! And according to the U.S. Department of Education, academic achievement drops sharply for children who watch television more than 10 hours a week. Time seems to mushroom as sitcom follows sitcom. So be attentive to the amount of time your child spends in front of the boob tube.

Just Turn It Off!

◆

According to the U.S. Department of Education, three factors over which parents exercise authority explain nearly 90 percent of the difference in eighth grade mathematics test scores across 37 states and the District of Columbia on the National Assessment of Educational Process (NAEP) test: student absenteeism, variety of reading materials in the home, and excessive television-watching.

What precisely is wrong with television for children? For one thing, there are all those lost hours. But most parents also recognize that what their children absorb is usually less than elevating. According to the Cultural Indicators Project of the Annenberg School of Communication at the University of Pennsylvania, the average American child will have witnessed more than 8,000 murders and 100,000 violent acts on television by the time he leaves elementary school, and some 40,000 murders and 200,000 acts of violence before leaving high school.

In addition, a barrage of recent important findings directly link television viewing with depression. People are hardwired to seek out challenges. Passive couch-potatoing runs counter to our natural inclinations, especially with young people. So don't be surprised when your children are antsy, miserable, and unpleasant after several hours of passive, listless television viewing.

In fairness, we also need to acknowledge that children see much else besides—television is not all shoot-outs. They laugh to cheerful comedies, get caught up in the thrill of sports, participate in the season's hottest dramas, and even pay an occasional visit to an "educational" program. Do these milder, less-offensive shows offset the more offensive programs? Probably not. And where does this concern with television leave parents who want to know how much viewing time is appropriate for their children? Probably in the living room in front of the tube. Children may watch a lot of television, but so do grown-ups. In fact, more than a third of America's free time is devoted to television; that's four times more than the next leisure activity and more hours than the next 10 highest-ranked leisure time activities put together. (This choice of leisure activity is increasingly global. According to current estimates, people on the planet spend nearly 4 billion hours watching television every day!)

At the risk of repeating ourselves, if there is one big favor you can do to help your child's education, it's limiting the amount of television he or she watches. You can expect an increase in your child's tests scores as a result. This is, of course, easier said than done—television is such a central part of so many lives. But if you are serious about your children's education, you *will* limit the amount of television watched in your house.

Begin by setting boundaries. No television before homework is completed is one reasonable rule. No more than an hour of TV—preferably less—on a school night is another reasonable regulation. (Yes, of course, there are exceptions. But exceptions too often and too quickly become the rule.) Special programs, by the way, can be taped for viewing on the weekend when your child will have more free time.

You do, dear parent, have a legitimate say in what your child watches. You might begin the week reviewing together with your child upcoming programs. Discuss the pros and cons of what to see and point out educational programs that seem entertaining and interesting. Allow your child appropriate latitude in making choices, but keep an eye on the time allotted for these selected programs.

Rethinking television can't be solely an issue for the children—it must be a decision for the whole family. What will you and the kids do when the set is turned off? And will you do it together?

THE PLEASURES OF SHARED EXPERIENCES

When was the last time you took your child to a museum? Bet it's been too long. How about a trip to the public library? The concert hall? As are most parents, no doubt you, too, are time-deprived and don't have the luxury of visiting cultural institutions as often as you'd like. True, but we bet you could find a free afternoon here and there if you put your mind to it.

Where should you go? What activities are the most effective? The key is to do things that you enjoy personally because there is no better inspiration to a child than a parent's genuine delight in learning or art. Take in a concert, spend the evening in the living room reading, bring charity to a penny harvest. Dream together. What could be a more gratifying experience for a parent than to recapture the childhood pleasures of new learning experiences—and sharing the moment with one's own child?

Appendix A

◆

A Parent's Directory of Web Sites

The World Wide Web is a terrific—and dynamic—source of information about standardized tests. Your state's Department of Education web site will have the latest information about local standardized testing programs. Web sites maintained by national test publishers contain information about specific test products and are likely to have well-chosen links to test-related resources. Web sites supported by the government, universities, and advocacy groups also provide useful information about testing.

Here, then, is an annotated list of our favorite web sites, arranged by category.

TESTING INFORMATION RESOURCES

TIMSS, Third International Mathematics and Science Study
   http://wwwcsteep.bc.edu/timss
TIMSS is an international achievement test that measures student achievement in science. This web site contains information about

the TIMSS testing program, the scope of material tested, how achievement is measured, which countries participate in the study, what information is collected, and an overview of the results.

Educational Testing Service
http://www.ets.org

The Educational Testing Service (ETS) is a private, nonprofit organization that supports educational measurement and research and develops standardized tests for a variety of public and private clients, including The College Board, creators of the SAT. This site offers a special area for parents that contains some excellent information about testing and education issues.

National Assessment of Educational Progress
http://www.nces.ed.gov/naep

This site provides an overview of the annual National Assessment of Educational Progress testing program, a project that tracks U.S. student achievement in a wide range of subjects.

Consortium for Equity in Standards and Testing (CTEST)
http://wwwcsteep.bc.edu/ctest

This web site contains an incredible range of information and resources on standards and testing, many of which are designed especially for parents. The Consortium's mission is to "focus attention on how educational standards, assessments, and tests can be used more fairly."

FairTest
http://www.fairtest.org

The National Center for Fair & Open Testing (FairTest) is an advocacy organization that works to educate the public about issues related to standardized testing and to press for assessment programs that are fair, open, and educationally sound.

ERIC® Clearinghouse on Assessment and Evaluation

http://ericae.net

The ERIC® (Educational Resources Information Center) Clearinghouse on Assessment and Evaluation contains links to hundreds of assessment-related resources. Its stated goals are to provide balanced information about educational assessment and to encourage responsible test use. Within this site is a link to the central ERIC® web site, which will link you to current information and research on just about any education-related topic you can think of.

National Center for Research on Evaluation, Standards, and Student Testing (CRESST)

http://cresst96.cse.ucla.edu/index.htm

The National Center for Research on Evaluation, Standards, and Student Testing is affiliated with UCLA's Graduate School of Education & Information Studies and conducts research on a wide range of important topics related to K-12 educational testing. The CRESST web site contains practical and academic information about testing and assessment.

CRESST Information for Parents

http://www.cresst96.cse.ucla.edu/parenta.htm#Glossary

This site is part of the main CRESST web site, and contains links to a wide range of assessment-related materials that are directed specifically at parents.

The College Board

www.collegeboard.org

The College Board is a national membership association (members include high schools and colleges/universities) that aims to facilitate student transition to higher education. The College Board is a source of programs, services, and information in the areas of assessment, guidance, admission, placement, financial aid, curriculum, and research. If you're thinking ahead to your child's high school experience—and the standardized tests that he or she will be facing on the road to college—this is a great site to check out.

Test Publishers/Testing Companies

CTB/McGraw-Hill

http://www.ctb.com

CTB/McGraw-Hill is the nation's largest publisher of norm-referenced examinations, criterion-referenced examinations, and instructional management programs for elementary and secondary schools. The TerraNova/Comprehensive Test of Basic Skills is the most popular of its commercial testing products. CTB has a wide range of such products and is commonly engaged by individual states to develop state-specific assessment instruments. This site contains information about CTB test products as well as links to a variety of useful education and assessment-related sites.

Harcourt Brace Educational Measurement

http://www.hbem.com

Harcourt Brace Educational Measurement develops and markets assessment products and related materials and services for elementary, secondary, and higher education. Popular products include the Stanford Achievement Test Series, which was the first norm-referenced achievement test, the Metropolitan Achievement Test, and the Otis-Lennon School Ability Test.

Houghton Mifflin Company/Riverside

http://www.hmco.com/hmco/riverside

At this site, you can learn more about Riverside Publishing's most popular assessment products, including the Iowa Tests of Basic Skills and the Cognitive Abilities Test (CogAT). It is one of the country's largest developers and publishers of student assessment instruments and has recently expanded its core business to include custom development of criterion-referenced tests for Arizona, Michigan, New Jersey, Ohio, and Washington, among other states.

Education Resources

Education Week on the Web

http://www.edweek.org

Education Week, published by a non-profit organization called Editorial Projects in Education, is "America's Educaton Newspaper of Record." Its web site presents an on-line version of each week's edition as well as access to archival articles and material. This site is a terrific source of information on educational issues in general—with daily updates, in-depth special reports, access to the on-line version of *Teacher* magazine, and a well-designed search engine.

Council of Chief State School Officers (CCSSO)

http://www.ccsso.org

The CCSSO is a national non-profit organization that represents and supports the public officials who lead state Departments of Education in the U.S. Its focus is on primary and secondary education. Among its activities is a wide range of research projects that focus on nationwide education issues; each year, the CCSSO conducts an in-depth survey of state standardized testing programs and makes the results available to the general public.

Education Commission of the States

www.ecs.org

The Education Commission of the States works to support Governors and other state officials in their efforts to improve education for all children by sponsoring networks, organizing conferences, conducting research, and publishing research reports and maintaining an information clearinghouse. This site is interesting because it can give you an overview of national education issues along with access to specific assessment-related resources.

ParentsPlace

http://www.parentsplace.com

This is a commercial web site that provides parents with information, helpful hints, and useful tips on a wide range of parenting-related resources. While education is but one of many areas that this site focuses on, the information it provides is valuable. It also has an excellent search feature, which allows you to search the entire ParentsPlace site for relevant information on standardized testing and education.

Educational Resources Information Center (ERIC®)

www.aspensys.com/eric/index.html

ERIC is a comprehensive, searchable database of education-related research findings, practical information, and academic scholarship. According to its mission statement, "… the mission of the ERIC system is to improve American education by increasing and facilitating the use of educational research and information to effect good practice in the activities of learning, teaching, educational decision-making, and research, wherever and whenever these activities take place." One of the best ERIC resources is its searchable database of ERIC Digests, which are short (2-page) articles about education-related topics. The Digest database contains more than 1,600 of these documents, each providing useful syntheses of current trends in educational research and theory.

ERIC® Publications for Parents

www.ed.gov/pubs/parents.html

This site, a sub-site of the ERIC database, provides a direct link to education resources that are geared toward parents.

American Educational Research Association (AERA)

http://www.aera.net

The AERA, an association of scholarly researchers in education and related areas, directs its efforts toward "improving the educational process by encouraging scholarly inquiry related to education and by promoting the dissemination and practical application of research results." The AERA sponsors national conferences for education researchers and serves as an international professional organization for its members, promoting their work. Many of the resources here are scholarly in nature and provide access to the latest research on testing and assessment.

Family Education Network

http://www.familyeducation.com/index.asp

This advertiser-supported site is a great resource for parents who want to be a positive influence on their child's education. It contains links to printed resources, access to on-line "experts," and links to other education-related web sites.

National Parent Teacher Association

http://www.pta.org

The National PTA is the largest volunteer association in the United States working exclusively on behalf of children and youth. It does advocacy work, supports legislative activity, and supports parents, nationwide, in their efforts to improve and support education. This site contains a vast array of education-related resources, accessible through well-designed links and a strong search engine.

National School Boards Association

http://www.nsba.org

The National School Boards Association works to promote "… excellence and equity in public education through school board leadership." This site is primarily devoted to education policy, local school governance issues, and a wide range of practical information on school-related issues, including testing and assessment.

National Parent Education Network

http://www.npin.org

The National Parent Education Network, an ERIC-sponsored project, collects and disseminates information on education-related topics to parents. This searchable database is an excellent resource for parents interested in gathering information about testing and assessment.

Association for Supervision and Curriculum Development (ASCD)
    http://www.ascd.org
The ASCD is an international, non-profit, non-partisan organization that represents teachers, principals, and other education professionals in their efforts to support successful learning for all. The ASCD provides professional development resources in curriculum and supervision and promotes educational equity for all students. Although not directed specifically at parents, the site contains education-related resources that may be of use.

Government Resources

U.S. Department of Education
    www.ed.gov
The U.S. Department of Education's web site is a terrific resource for parents. Not only does it contain important information about current education policy, trends, and research, but it also provides Internet links to many other education web sites. From this site, you can access ERIC, the National Center for Education Statistics (NCES), the National Parent Education Network (NPIN), and your state Department of Education.

National Center for Education Statistics
    http://www.nces.ed.gov
The National Center for Education Statistics collects and reports "… statistics and information showing the condition and progress of education in the United States and other nations in order to promote and accelerate the improvement of American education." The NCES studies cover the entire educational spectrum, providing the facts and figures needed to help policymakers understand the condition of education in the nation today, to give researchers needed data, and to help teachers and administrators decide on the best practices for their schools.

This site contains information, research reports, and statistics on just about any education-related topic imaginable. From this site, you can link to the National Assessment of Educational Progress (NAEP) web site, which contains information about this annual national test of student achievement and progress.

North Central Regional Educational Lab (NCREL)

http://www.ncrel.org

The North Central Regional Educational Laboratory (NCREL) is one of 10 regional educational laboratories. NCREL provides research-based resources and assistance to educators, policymakers, and communities in Illinois, Indiana, Iowa, Michigan, Minnesota, Ohio, and Wisconsin. On the web, however, its vast resources are accessible to parents in any state. While this site does not focus specifically on assessment issues, the site's search engine will direct you to many resources that do.

Midwest Continent Regional Educational Lab (McREL)

www.mcrel.org

Like NCREL, McREL is one of 10 regional educational laboratories that provide schools, teachers, and communities with first-rate products, professional development resources, and service.

State Departments of Education

State Department of Education web sites are as diverse as the states they serve. Each site will, however, provide you with in-depth information about current education policies and programs in your state—and give you specific information about whom to contact (via phone, e-mail, or regular mail) if you wish to receive additional information that is not available on the web.

Quick link to any state:

ericps.ed.uiuc.edu/eece/statlink.html

Or go directly to your state:

Alabama
www.alsde.edu/

Alaska
www.educ.state.ak.us/

Arizona
ade.state.az.us/doe.html

Arkansas
arkedu.state.ar.us/

California
goldmine.cde.ca.gov/

Colorado
www.cde.state.co.us

Connecticut
www.state.ct.us/sde/

Delaware
www.k12.de.us/k12/default.htm

District of Columbia
www.k12.dc.us/

Florida
www.firn.edu/doe/

Georgia
www.doe.k12.ga.us/

Hawaii
  kalama.doe.hawaii.edu/upena/

Idaho
  www.sde.state.id.us/Dept/

Illinois
  www.isbe.state.il.us/

Indiana
  doe.state.in.us/

Iowa
  www.state.ia.us/educate/depteduc/

Kansas
  www.ksbe.state.ks.us/

Kentucky
  www.kde.state.ky.us/

Louisiana
  www.doe.state.la.us/

Maine
  www.state.me.us/education/

Maryland
  www.msde.state.md.us/

Massachusetts
  www.doe.mass.edu/

Michigan
  www.mde.state.mi.us/

Minnesota
www.educ.state.mn.us/

Mississippi
mdek12.state.ms.us/

Missouri
services.dese.state.mo.us/

Montana
161.7.114.15/opi/opi.html

Nebraska
nde4.nde.state.ne.us/

Nevada
www.nsn.k12.nv.us/nvdoe/

New Hampshire
www.state.nh.us/doe/education.html

New Jersey
www.state.nj.us/education

New Mexico
de.state.nm.us/

New York
www.nysed.gov/

North Carolina
www.dpi.state.nc.us/

North Dakota
www.dpi.state.nd.us/

Ohio
www.ode.ohio.gov/

Oklahoma
sde.state.ok.us/

Oregon
www.ode.state.or.us//

Pennsylvania
www.cas.psu.edu/pde.html

Rhode Island
instruct.ride.ri.net/ride_home_page.html

South Carolina
www.state.sc.us/sde/

South Dakota
www.state.sd.us/state/executive/deca/

Tennessee
www.state.tn.us/education/

Texas
www.tea.state.tx.us/

Utah
www.usoe.k12.ut.us/

Vermont
www.cit.state.vt.us/educ/

Virginia
pen.k12.va.us/Anthology/VDOE/

Washington
www.ospi.wednet.edu/

West Virginia
wvde.state.wv.us/

Wisconsin
www.dpi.state.wi.us/

Wyoming
www.k12.wy.us/wdehome.html

Appendix B

◆

A Parent's Directory of Resources for Children with Learning Disabilities

This appendix lists several organizations where you can find specific information about learning disabilities. These resources will help you understand the issues that affect the schooling of your child—for example, your child's legal right to an education and the accommodations that he may need in the classroom.

These organizations also provide specific information about the standardized testing criteria in your state. Since criteria and procedures vary by school district, it's important to familiarize yourself with the information provided by your state and local agencies. The following contacts should be able to help you locate sources of information and support.

Resources about Learning Disabilities

Family Village: A Global Community of Disability-Related
Resources
Waisman Center
University of Wisconsin-Madison
1500 Highland Avenue
Madison, WI 53705-2280
e-mail: rowley@waisman.wisc.edu
web site: http://familyvillage.wisc.edu

The Family Village integrates information, resources, and communications on the Internet for persons with disabilities and their families. The web site offers a forum for parents to discuss with other parents their shared concerns relating to their children's disability.

ERIC® Clearinghouse on Disabilities and Gifted Education
1920 Association Drive
Reston, VA 22091-1589
800-328-0272
e-mail: ericec@cec.sped.org
web site: http://www.cec.sped.org/ericec.htm

The ERIC® Clearinghouse on Disabilities and Gifted Education is a federally funded database containing over 900,000 items regarding children with disabilities. It's a great resource for specific information about various disabilities and ways to support your learning-disabled child.

National Information Center for Children and Youth with
Disabilities (NICHCY)
P.O. Box 1492
Washington, DC 20013-1492
800-695-0285
202-884-8200
web site: http://www.nichcy.org/index.html

NICHCY is a national information and referral center that provides information on disabilities and disability-related issues for families, educators, and other professionals. Their special focus is children and youth (birth to age 22).

Learning Disabilities Association of America (LDA)

4156 Library Road
Pittsburgh, PA 15234
412-341-1515

The LDA is the largest non-profit volunteer advocacy group for individuals with learning disabilities. LDA has 50 state affiliates and more than 600 local chapters in 50 states, Washington DC, and Puerto Rico. The LDA membership—composed of individuals with learning disabilities, family members, and concerned professionals—serves as advocates for the more than two million students of school age with learning disabilities as well as adults with learning disabilities.

National Center for Learning Disabilities (NCLD)

99 Park Avenue, 6th Floor
New York, NY 10016
212-687-7211
web site: http://www.ncld.org

The National Center for Learning Disabilities is one of the foremost national not-for-profit organizations committed to improving the lives of those affected by learning disabilities. NCLD's mission is to promote public awareness and understanding of children and adults with learning disabilities while providing national leadership on their behalf.

Resources Concerning Specific Disabilities

Children and Adults with Attention Deficit Disorders (CH.A.D.D.)

499 North West 70th Avenue, Suite 101
Plantation, FL 33317
954-587-3700

Your Legal Rights:
Individuals with Disabilities Education Act

◆

Public Law 101-476, popularly known as IDEA, defines the rights of children with disabilities and their parents. A basic provision of the law is the right of parents to participate in the educational decision-making process. This means that you have a right to take part in the development of your child's Individualized Education Program (IEP), which is a written statement of the educational program designed to meet your child's unique needs. The IEP also stipulates which services the school will provide to help your child's education. These services may include testing accommodations and modifications to help your child when taking standardized tests.

For questions about IDEA and the legal protection it offers for your child, contact:

Office of Special Education Programs (OSEP)
Contact Person: Rhonda Weiss (202) 205-9053

Office of Special Education and Rehabilitative Services (OSERS)
Contact Person: Amy Bennett (202) 205-8555

Office of Civil Rights, U.S. Department of Education
Contact Person: Karen Hakel (202) 205-9036

Deaf and hearing-impaired individuals may call:
(202) 205-5465 or (800) 358-8247 for TDD Services

CH.A.D.D. is the nation's leading non-profit organization for children and adults with attention deficit disorders. This is a good resource for tips on how to help and support your ADD child both at school and at home.

National Attention Deficit Disorder Association (ADDA)
P.O. Box 488
West Newbury, MA 01985
800-487-2282
web site: http://add.org

The National Attention Deficit Disorder Association's mission is to help people with ADD lead happier, more successful lives through education, research, and public advocacy. ADDA focuses especially on the needs of young adults with ADD but also offers useful information to parents of children with ADD.

Orton Dyslexia Society
724 York Road
Baltimore, MD 21204
800-222-3123

The Orton Dyslexia Society is committed to helping children, youth, and adults with dyslexia. They support ongoing research on the disorder and make the information available to the public by means of newsletters and other publications.

Appendix C

◆

A Parent's Directory of CD-ROMs

This appendix presents an annotated list of some 20 CD-ROMs that will help prepare your child for success in the classroom and on standardized tests. As you are probably well aware, children are fascinated with the interactive world of computers. They can spend hours in front of the monitor, zapping monsters, building castles, interacting more closely with visiting aliens than they do with you. These games can enhance many different learning skills: math computation, writing, critical thinking, logical reasoning, problem solving, scientific processing, and memory tasks. The CD-ROMs listed here are sometimes classified as "edu-tainment," incorporating learning and fun.

To use this software, your computer must be properly equipped. You'll need a system with a CD-ROM disk drive and sufficient memory capacity—most new CD-ROMs feature complex graphics and animation that require lots of memory to run properly, so check to see if you have adequate memory.

CD-ROMs generally retail for $25-$50 and you'll probably want several for your collection, so select carefully. Make sure to pay attention to the age ranges provided by the publisher—the last thing you want to do is purchase a CD-ROM that your child will not use because it's "too easy" or "too boring." Be aware, too, that the ages listed on the CD box are only general guidelines; if your child is five but shows signs of exceptional talent in math, say, it would probably be wise to skip *James Discovers Math*, which is intended for children ages 3-6. You'd be better off in this case purchasing a program targeted for older children that your precocious child will grow into as she develops her mathematical skills.

Here are some of our favorite CDs, classified by subject matter, that make learning fun.

Math

James Discovers Math
Publisher: Broderbund
Operating System & Media: Windows
Topic: Math basic concepts and skills
Ages: 3-6
    James Discovers Math is an introduction to math for early learners. There are 10 lively activity areas within James's kitchen. All your child needs to do is click on the items in the kitchen to open up each game. She'll learn basic math concepts as she plays.

Pooh Ready for Math
Publisher: Disney
Operating System & Media: Macintosh and Windows
Topic: Beginning Math Skills
Ages: 3-6
    Disney's *Pooh Ready for Math* is a fun way to introduce math to young children. As they explore the 100 Acre Wood with Pooh, Tigger, and their friends, they choose from seven fun activities that teach and reinforce math skills ranging from counting and number-forming to beginning addition and subtraction.

Sesame Street: Numbers
Publisher: Electronic Arts
Operating System & Media: Macintosh and Windows
Topic: Math Readiness Skills; Counting
Ages: 3-6

Pre-schoolers get a lively introduction to math skills on Sesame Street with Elmo, Big Bird, Bert & Ernie, and, of course, the Count. The Sesame Street characters verbally guide children through four main math activities focusing on key aspects of math readiness, number recognition, set classification, counting, and spatial relationships of "near" and "far."

School Mega Math Blaster
Publisher: Davidson School Products
Operating System & Media: Macintosh and Windows
Topic: Math
Ages: 6-12

School Mega Math Blaster is the new and improved version of the original *Math Blaster* that children have loved for years. Aliens, spaceships, and asteroids threaten earth, and it's up to your child to use math to save the planet. The level of difficulty increases as questions are answered correctly, providing kids with a fun way of drilling the basic math skills that are necessary for success on standardized tests.

Math Workshop
Publisher: Broderbund
Operating System & Media: Macintosh and Windows
Topic: Critical Math Skills
Ages: 6-12

Math Workshop provides children with opportunities to learn, practice, and improve critical math skills. The program features an engaging environment filled with games, music, and animated characters that make learning fun. Each activity includes multiple levels of difficulty designed to reinforce confidence and motivation.

Aladdin Math Quest

Publisher: Disney
Operating System & Media: Macintosh and Windows
Topic: Basic Math through Introductory Geometry
Ages: 7-9

Aladdin Math Quest, featuring Robin Williams as "Genie," presents a challenging journey in which math is the key to saving the exotic land of Agrabah from the evil genie Bizarrah. Kids are encouraged by Genie and Iago to navigate through 18 challenging activities that build addition, subtraction, geometry, and other essential math skills as they progress in their quest. Multiple levels of difficulty keep the excitement alive and keep children coming back again and again.

The software was designed with the help of the noted math educator Marilyn Burns, and all activities address the standards set by the National Council of Teachers of Mathematics.

Test-Taking Skills: Games that Build Critical Thinking and Logical Reasoning

Mixed Up Mother Goose

Publisher: Sierra On-Line
Operating System & Media: Macintosh and Windows
Topic: Basic Organizational and Logic Skills
Ages: 3-6

Mixed Up Mother Goose is an animated adventure that introduces young children to computers while teaching them basic organizational and logic skills. Children go on an interactive journey to help sort out "Mixed Up Rhymes"—and have loads of fun in the process.

Bill Nye the Science Guy: Stop the Rock

Publisher: Disney
Operating System & Media: Macintosh and Windows

Topic: Scientific Problem Solving

Ages: 6 and up

In *Stop the Rock*, kids are challenged to stop a gigantic meteoroid speeding toward earth. Bill Nye, the Science Guy, leads the way to solve the seven tricky science riddles that will trigger MAAX, the diabolically smart computer network, who alone can destroy the meteoroid. Along the way, kids meet silly but smart scientists who teach them about real science, using high-powered science equipment. This program is a great way to build and reinforce knowledge of science as well as develop problem-solving skills.

101 Dalmations Escape from De Vil Manor

Publisher: Disney

Operating System & Media: Macintosh and Windows

Topic: Critical Thinking Skills

Ages: 6 and up

101 Dalmations is an interactive adventure game with leading-edge animation and a 3-D environment. Children will be thrilled with the innovative "Puppyvision" feature that puts them in the heart of the action as they become Patches, a dalmation puppy. They will be challenged to think and act like a puppy to solve puzzles and games. The game increases in difficulty, encouraging kids to think of different strategies to free the puppies from the evil Cruella De Vil.

Operation Neptune

Publisher: The Learning Company

Operating System & Media: Macintosh and Windows

Topic: Math Problem-Solving Skills

Ages: 9 and up

In this problem-solving adventure, kids get to pilot submarines as they try to stop underwater sea creatures from doing harm. Questions must be read, making the program a useful tool in building reading comprehension skills. Kids will be thrilled to solve the math problems by shooting these sea creatures with ink pellets!

Playtime in the Park
Publisher: Nova
Operating System & Media: Macintosh and Windows
Topic: Memory, Concentration, and Related Skills
Ages: 3-7

Playtime in the Park offers your child a chance to join the Bear Family on an enchanting journey through the park, exploring, learning, and making lots of friends along the way. The game builds memory and concentration, word-picture association, counting, hand-eye coordination, spelling, and creative thinking skills. Developing these skills early will increase your child's academic achievement as well as his ability to perform well on standardized tests.

SimTown
Publisher: Maxis
Operating System & Media: Macintosh and Windows
Topics: Planning, Problem-Solving, and Decision-Making Skills
Ages: 8-12

From the makers of the award-winning *SimCity*, *SimTown* lets kids build and manage a small town and influence the lives of the people who live there. As the town grows, resources are used and garbage is produced, giving kids an opportunity to understand and control the environmental effects of real-life neighborhoods. *SimTown* also challenges children with the consequences of dealing with large-scale problems and broad decision making.

Widget Workshop
Publisher: Maxis
Operating System & Media: Macintosh and Windows
Topic: Critical Thinking Skills
Ages: 8 and above

Widget Workshop turns kids into inventors by putting them in a laboratory setting with hundreds of fun and realistic objects. The challenge is to use simulated mechanical parts and pieces, such as light switches, gravity chambers, and even pulsing hearts, to connect objects in different ways. Kids can then design and construct their own science experiments or inventions or solve pre-built puzzles. Once their inventions are built, children can create self-running versions and share them with friends!

Zurk's Rainforest Lab

Publisher: Maxis
Operating System & Media: Macintosh and Windows
Topic: Science, Math, and Critical Thinking Skills
Ages: 5-9

This award-winning program teaches science, math, and critical thinking skills while introducing children to three languages: Spanish, French, and English. Kids explore the rainforest, classify animals, take pictures, write a story about their experience, complete pattern puzzles using geometry, and animate a "cursor-cub" in the framework of beautiful graphics. This software is a great opportunity for kids to develop their problem-solving abilities in a fun atmosphere of Latin music and surprising sounds.

Where in the World Is Carmen Sandiego?

Publisher: Broderbund
Operating System & Media: DOS, Macintosh, and Windows
Topic: Geography and History; Critical Thinking Skills
Ages: 8 and above

The best-selling *Where in the World Is Carmen Sandiego?* Deluxe Edition turns geography and history into an exciting detective chase incorporating music and sound effects as well as animation. Carmen and her original gang of nine villains—plus 10 new recruits—are stealing the treasures of the world. Children use critical thinking to piece together the clues to locate and stop Carmen. This software incorporates digitized slides provided by the National Geographic Society to help children learn about the locations profiled.

Language Arts: Reading and Writing Skills

Dr. Seuss's ABC

Publisher: Broderbund

Operating System & Media: Macintosh and Windows
Topics: Alphabet Letters and Sight Words
Ages: 3-6

Young children will be delighted to learn the alphabet with Dr. Seuss and Living Books. There are more than 400 alphabetically inspired surprises hidden within the program. Izzy and Ichabod guide young readers through this action-packed title featuring Dr. Seuss's unique humor, rhymes, and illustrations.

Sesame Street: Letters

Publisher: Electronic Arts
Operating System & Media: Macintosh and Windows
Topic: Alphabet Letters and Sounds
Ages: 3-6

Sesame Street: Letters offers pre-schoolers a fun way to learn the alphabet on America's favorite street. Kids play interactive learning games that focus on letters as they romp through the neighborhood with Oscar and Telly, visiting the homes of Big Bird, Snuffy, and Bert and Ernie. They'll discover enchanted storybooks, enjoy over an hour's worth of classic Sesame Street songs and video, and even call their favorite characters on the phone. This software is an excellent way of building the basic phonic skills necessary to becoming a strong reader.

Living Books

Publisher: Broderbund
Operating System & Media: Macintosh and Windows
Topic: Reading Skills: Spelling, Writing, Word Recognition
Ages: 5 and up

Living Books are lively, animated stories that teach reading skills. Charming characters bring the stories to life by talking, moving, and dancing. Words and sentences are highlighted for children to follow along as the story is read aloud. Each living book comes with the original storybook from which it was adapted, including *Just Grandma & Me, Arthur's Teacher Troubles, Arthur's Birthday,* and *Ruff's Bone.*

Word Tales

Publisher: WEA
Operating System & Media: Macintosh and Windows
Topic: Alphabet and Vocabulary Skills
Ages: 4-7

Your child will have fun learning word recognition and initial letter sounds with these animated, interactive games. She'll be motivated to learn the alphabet and acquire vocabulary skills in a playful and fun atmosphere.

The Amazing Writing Machine

Publisher: Broderbund
Operating System & Media: Macintosh and Windows
Topic: Writing Skills
Ages: 6-12

The Amazing Writing Machine is a creative-writing, illustration, and idea-generating program that motivates kids to write. Children can express their thoughts, ideas, and opinions in five different writing forms: Story, Letter, Journal, Essay, and Poem, using colorful paint brushes, stamps, and drawing tools. For story ideas, kids can select from hundreds of "Bright Ideas" and then type to the sounds of drum beats and stampeding horses!

Glossary

The world of testing has developed its own jargon, and you need definitions to help you make your way through the maze. Here, then, is a glossary of key terms used by educators.

Achievement Test
A test designed to measure a student's skills or knowledge in a given subject area.

Age Norms
Scores, or values, that represent the average performance of students in a given age group.

Aptitude
A natural ability or capacity for learning. An aptitude test is a standardized instrument designed to measure the test-taker's ability to learn or acquire specific skills.

Attention Deficit Disorder (ADD)

This disorder results in a difficulty with focusing and maintaining attention. Children with ADD, as a result, are likely to have corresponding emotional and developmental problems both at home and in the school environment.

Average

The numerical score that represents the mathematical mean of a given set of scores of a given group of students. An average is calculated by adding all scores in a given set and dividing the sum by the number of test-takers.

Alignment

Alignment is the process of connecting classroom teaching, curriculum, and learning to assessments. These assessments are designed to reflect student knowledge and performance. This process involves several steps: (1) the creation of specific content and performance standards; (2) the development and implementation of these assessments; and (3) use of assessed standards to develop appropriate curricula and classroom teaching methods.

Alternative (Performance) Assessment

Alternative assessments ask students to respond with their own, original response to a question rather than to select a response from a set of choices. Questions posed in alternative assessments are typically open-ended—students are asked to design experiments, complete complex tasks, and use learned skills to solve real-world problems. Portfolios, oral responses, journals, and written responses are examples of the tasks or items used in alternative assessment.

Anchors

A sample of student work that typifies a specific level of performance. Anchors are necessary for performance or other authentic assessments, as they are the reference point against which scorers, or raters (teachers or professional test-scorers) gauge individual student performance on test questions.

Aptitude Test

An aptitude test is a test designed to measure students' capacity for learning or potential for achievement.

Assessment

The process by which the achievement, aptitude, or knowledge of a student or group of students is measured. Types of assessments include alternative, authentic, criterion-referenced, norm-referenced, and performance.

Battery

A group of related tests that are administered together to a group of students, and whose scores are reported, valued, and interpreted individually, in combination, and entirely.

Benchmark

A point of reference—a standard—against which performance can be measured. In an educational context, benchmarks represent detailed sets of knowledge and/or measures of performance expected of students at a given age, grade, or developmental level. Often, assessments are specifically designed to measure student performance in relation to statewide benchmarks, or standards; these tests fall into the category of criterion-referenced tests, as they measure performance against a specific set of criteria.

Ceiling

The upper limit of ability or performance that can be measured by a given test.

Classroom Assessment

Classroom assessments are tests created, implemented, and graded by a teacher (or group of teachers) in order to measure student performance on a given topic or mastery of a specific set of skills. Classroom tests are directly related to a student's performance in a given class with a given teacher; unlike standardized tests, classroom tests can be used to immediately measure student performance and to provide remediation or enrichment where necessary.

Cognitive Ability

Cognitive ability, as measured by standardized testing instruments, describes the level at which an individual is capable of thinking, learning, and/or knowing certain skills, concepts, or processes.

Content Standards

Expectations of what students should know or should be able to do in a given subject area at a given grade level. Increasingly, content standards are being used to inform and direct curriculum—to define what schools should teach when.

Criterion-Referenced Assessment

A test that measures a student's performance against a specific criteria or set of criteria or skills in terms of mastery level. The focus is on measuring an individual student's performance against a set of knowledge that he or she is or has been expected to learn.

Diagnostic Test

A test that is designed to measure a student's knowledge, skills, strengths, and weaknesses in a narrowly-defined subject area. Diagnostic tests are used to assess individual student performance and to determine his or her specific learning needs, for example, enrichment or remediation.

Dyslexia

A learning disability marked by difficulty in the understanding of language, including listening, speaking, reading, writing, and spelling. Dyslexia is often difficult to diagnose, and children who are eventually diagnosed may often have been diagnosed earlier with cognitive disabilities—but in fact, dyslexia does not necessarily mean that a child has cognitive difficulties, just that he or she has difficulty processing and outputting written material.

Equity

Equity, as it relates to standardized testing, is concerned with fairness—that is, making sure that assessments are free from bias. A fair assessment gives all students who take it an equal chance of having their performance measured accurately.

Grade Equivalent

The estimated grade-level that corresponds with a student's performance on a given assessment.

Individualized Educational Plan (IEP)

A written plan describing a specific educational program for an educationally disabled student.

Item

A specific, or individual, question in an assessment.

IQ

A number used to express the apparent relative intelligence of a person as determined by dividing his mental age—as determined by his performance on a standardized test—by his chronological age and multiplying it by 100. The Stanford-Binet Test is the most commonly used IQ test.

Limited English Proficiency (LEP)

A student classified as having LEP is deemed to have limited ability in English. However, there are no uniform criteria for what qualifies an individual for LEP status.

National Assessment of Educational Progress (NAEP)

The NAEP, administered by the federal government since the 1969-1970 school year, tracks the educational achievements of fourth, eighth, and twelfth grade students over time in selected content areas. At this time, very few students actually take part in the NAEP each year, as it is given to a nationwide sample of students.

National Percentile

A national percentile score represents a student's performance on a given test in relation to the performance of other students—nationwide (the national norm group)—at the same grade level who have taken the same test.

Norm

Standards, or scores, are established by a reference group and used to represent typical performance.

Norm Group

A group of students chosen to represent a certain population of students to whom a standardized test is administered with the aim of establishing performance norms. Norm groups may be broadly defined—for example, all fourth graders in the United States—or narrowly defined—all sixth graders attending private or independent schools in rural areas.

Percentile

A value on a scale of 1 to 100 that indicates the percent of a distribution that is equal to or below it. For example, a percentile score of 95 represents achievement that is equal to or better than 95 percent of the students taking the test.

Performance Standards

Specific definitions of what students must know, understand, accomplish, or do in order to demonstrate proficiency at a specific level as defined by benchmarks or content standards.

Portfolio Assessment

A portfolio is a collection of a student's classroom work. When a portfolio becomes subject to assessment, the contents are reviewed by a trained rater and are used to judge student performance. Portfolio assessment is most effective when the purpose and criteria of assessment are clearly established.

Published Test
A test that is publicly available.

Raw Score
The actual number of test items that are answered correctly.

Reliability
The degree to which the results of an assessment are dependable and consistent over time. Aspects of reliability include: between different administrations of the same test (retest reliability); between test items designed to measure the same skill or knowledge (item reliability); and between different raters (scorers) (rater reliability). If an assessment is unreliable, it cannot be valid.

Sample
A finite number of individuals in a given population (e.g., all fourth graders in the United States) that is assessed and whose performance is studied in order to gain information about the population as a whole.

Scale
Values that are assigned to represent different levels of student performance, usually in the context of an alternative (performance) assessment. Scaled scores—which combine a student's responses to a number of items—are used to place individual student performance along a continuum.

Standard Error of Measurement
Since any test has a certain (small) percentage of error built in to it, the standard error of measurement represents the estimated

amount of expected variability that is built in to a particular score on a particular test.

Standardized Test

A form of assessment that has been normed against a specific population, so that subsequent student performance on the test can be meaningfully scored and interpreted. Standardization is accomplished by first giving the test to a sample group within a given population and then calculating scores, means, standard deviations, and percentiles. When an individual student takes a standardized test, his or her scores can be compared meaningfully with the norm group's performance.

Standards

Statements of expectations for student learning, performance, and/or knowledge.

Standards-Based Reform

An approach to school reform that involves setting high content and performance standards for all students—and then adapting instruction and assessment in such a way that all students have an equal opportunity to meet the high standards.

Stanine

One of the nine classes into which a set of normalized standard scores arranged according to rank in educational testing are divided. The first stanine (1) contains the bottom 4% of scores, the ninth stanine (9) contains the top 4% of scores, and the middle stanine (5) contains the middle 20% of scores. The remaining scores are distributed, according to their percentile, among the rest of the stanine rankings.

Third International Mathematics and Science Study (TIMSS)

TIMSS is an international test of mathematics and science ability and knowledge administered to students around the world at ages 9 and 13 and in the last year of high school (or its equivalent). Currently, in the United States, students are tested in the fourth, eighth, and twelfth grades. TIMSS at this time is given only to a sample of students nationwide. Although TIMSS measures student performance, its main purpose is to assess mathematics and science curriculum, because it is based on the premise that "curriculum and teaching methods help determine what we learn."

Validity
The extent to which a test measures what it was intended to measure.

Index

About the Authors

Peter W. Cookson, Jr., Ph.D., is Director of the Center for Educational Outreach and Innovation at Teachers College Columbia University, the world's foremost graduate school of education. Dr. Cookson is the co-author of eight books, including *School Choice and the Struggle for the Soul of American Education.*

Joshua Halberstam, Ph.D., is a visiting scholar at New York University and is on the staff of the Center for Educational Outreach and Innovation at Teachers College. He is the author of *Everyday Ethics: Inspired Solutions to Real-Life Dilemmas* and several other books that deftly distill complicated issues for a mass audience.

Kristina Berger, an experienced tutor and teacher of standardized test-taking skills, holds a MA from Teachers College Columbia University and has many years' experience developing educational programs for children and teachers.

Susan A. Mescavage taught at the elementary level in both independent and public schools for several years and holds a Master of Education degree from Teachers College Columbia University, where she is now pursuing a doctorate of education in educational administration.

The LearningExpress Web Site

◆

Parents looking for the very best in basic skills resources should visit the LearningExpress web site at *www.learnx.com*. Whether your child needs improvement in math, spelling, reading, study habits, or reasoning skills, LearningExpress can help. You'll find dozens of books designed to help build skills vital for standardized tests and classroom success through fun, easy exercises and friendly instruction. Visit us today!